The Hand of God and a Few Bright Flowers

The Hand of God
and a Few Bright Flowers

Poems by William Olsen

UNIVERSITY OF ILLINOIS PRESS   Urbana and Chicago

Acknowledgment is made to the following publications where some of these poems appeared, sometimes in different versions:

Antioch Review: "To Darwin Reading the Bible"
Black Warrior Review: "The Short-Order Cook" (now "From the Boss Hotel")
Crazyhorse: "Mockingbirds," "The Only Neighborhood," "The Unicorn Tapestries," "Saint Paul the Hermit, Saint Anthony, and the Pipistrelles"
Domestic Crude: "Nostalgie du Mal"
Gulf Coast Magazine: "December"
Hayden's Ferry Review: "Eighteen Species of Hummingbirds"
Ironwood: "Mr. and Mrs. Samuel McCall"
The Nation: "Public Gardens," "Vocations"
New Orleans Review: "Addressing His Deaf Wife, Kansas, 1908"
The New Republic: "Breughel's Peasants and the Month of August"
North American Review: "Mules in a Field"
Poetry Northwest: "The Leeches," "Wherever It Goes, Wherever You Go," "The Dead Monkey," "Water"
Seattle Review: "*In Situ* outside Petrograd"
Shenandoah: "In Memory of Jean Rhys," "Tomorrow"
Sonora Review: "Envy," "There Are Many Boats," "Trees"
Telescope: "Over and Under the Sun"
Tendril: "Five Years"

"Addressing His Deaf Wife, Kansas, 1908" was reprinted in *The Anthology of Magazine Verse and Yearbook of American Poetry,* 1981. "In Memory of Jean Rhys" was reprinted in *New Voices 1979–1983* (selections by May Swenson), Academy of American Poets.

Some of these poems appeared in *Flight*, a pamphlet published by San Pedro Press.

Library of Congress Cataloging-in-Publication Data

Olsen, William, 1954–
The hand of God and a few bright flowers : poems / by William Olsen.
p.   cm.
ISBN 0-252-06001-6 (alk. paper)
I. Title.
PS3565.L822H3   1988
811'.54—dc19   87-24507
                         CIP

The National Poetry Series

The National Poetry Series was established in 1978 to publish five collections of poetry annually through five participating publishers. The manuscripts are selected by five poets of national reputation. Publication is funded by James A. Michener, Edward J. Piszek, The Copernicus Society of America, The National Endowment for the Arts, The Friends of the National Poetry Series, and the five publishers— E. P. Dutton, Graywolf Press, William Morrow & Co., Persea Books, and the University of Illinois Press.

1987

The Singing Underneath by Jeffrey Harrison
Selected by James Merrill. E. P. Dutton & Company.

The Good Thief by Marie Howe
Selected by Margaret Atwood. Persea Books.

The Hand of God and a Few Bright Flowers by William Olsen
Selected by David Wagoner. University of Illinois Press.

A Guide to Forgetting by Jeffrey Skinner
Selected by Tess Gallagher. Graywolf Press.

New Math by Leigh Cole Swensen
Selected by Michael Palmer. William Morrow & Company.

FOR NANCY EIMERS

Contents

I.

The Unicorn Tapestries   3

Wherever It Goes, Wherever You Go   4

Tomorrow   5

Vocations   8

From the Boss Hotel   11

The Only Neighborhood   13

Trees   14

Nostalgie du Mal   15

There Are Many Boats   16

The World's Despite   18

II.

Breughel's Peasants and the Month of August   25

Mules in a Field   26

Saint Paul the Hermit, Saint Anthony, and the Pipistrelles 28

In Situ outside Petrograd   30

Addressing His Deaf Wife, Kansas, 1908   32

Mr. and Mrs. Samuel McCall   33

The Hand of God and a Few Bright Flowers   34

To Darwin Reading the Bible   38

The Leeches   39

III.

Mockingbirds   45

In Memory of Jean Rhys   46

The Dead Monkey   49

Over and Under the Sun   51

Envy 54

December 56

Five Years 58

Water 59

Eighteen Species of Hummingbirds 61

Public Gardens 63

For every thing exists and not one sigh nor smile nor tear
Nor hair nor particle of dust, not one can pass away.

    — BLAKE

I.

The Unicorn Tapestries

The things we leave behind must, for those
who find them flattened, scentless inside books
or in a gesture they make that isn't theirs,
be very much like the desk I found in the alley
one night, coming out of one way down another,

when I couldn't sleep or write letters, and walked.
The desk had lost a leg, and couldn't get away.
Some initials cut through oak had outlasted love.
Turning over the drawer to interpret
the contents, I thought of the farmer centuries ago
and the stack of "curtains" he found in a chest.
All the crazy things he couldn't understand—

the unicorn, Christ reborn; the seductive
damsel, Mary, who lured Him into the circular fence,
Her dress lifted ever so slightly, Her glance askew,
His smiling as if all the world centered on Him,
a field of lilies, violets, passionate roses
and periwinkles, "joy of the ground"—

he took them to the barn to cover the potatoes.
Little worked that winter. The potatoes darkened
the light that hid inside them. They grew eyes
until they were nothing but vision drained of life:
the unicorn bleeding and braying all winter
as the farmer lifted it and saw his work

ruined, for all his efforts.

Wherever It Goes, Wherever You Go

I want to talk about what must succeed
the small miracle of catching a bus.
Once I was heaved up into the midst of talk
while people clutched the metal poles and seemed
to surf somewhere between their work and homes.
The wet streets burned more eternally than these citizens
stepping off into the night, and it was all
the bus driver could do to smile behind
his voice that said *have a good evening*
with the irony that helps us live our lives
and sometimes lives our lives.
Suddenly in front of me the veins
of someone's neck flared with a force that had
no driver, only pain for destination.
She turned around and started screaming at me,
drank one long intensifying look,
then toppled on her face and gave another scream
for which there is no parallel. A businessman
put a pen in her mouth like a thermometer.
A nurse came forth, waved him off and said
you've got to let the tongue ungag itself.
And when the paramedics finally came
the old Chicano woman didn't have
any identification in her purse,
just handful after handful of used tissues
floating all around her like white blossoms.
Whatever monstrous thing I was that evening
wasn't what dropped her to the floor.
I'd been a pair of eyes to focus on
before my face became a window
to a staggering radiance
and she dropped to another time and place
than the tender hand moonwalking her neck,
before the sorrow of her life
closed down on us, who looked on mollified,
her face such a dilapidated house
anyone could stand being inside it but us.

Tomorrow

A water sprinkler empties into parabolas
which, before they collapse into the past,
hang in air unencumbered by the ones before,
each as irreplaceable as the gauzy streetlights
blossoming above the electric leaves
of the tall clouds of elms staring across the street.
Though it's midnight and the black material of being
crumbles between the tendril tips of stars
that poke and rummage through the compost of the summer sky,
as late as it is the old cop is sweeping
our common driveway, the sound of his labor
wearing as thin as the sucking tide of cars.
And every tomorrow comes down to the next
moment like the first green sticky hand-grenade
bud of spring about to explode into leaf.
Soon the trees have crowns, and the blue rugs of their
shadows. Then the first leaf kisses the ground
and scuttles on its rusted tips across our driveway
until the sycamores are bleached antlers in the sunlight.
But this occurs gradually, this neat, bare ascent to absence.
As it happens, the old cop gets knocked off on duty
many tomorrows ago, and many tomorrows later
it occurs to me I haven't seen him raking,
his bicycle tangled in morning glory vines,
and still more tomorrows later I started this poem
one morning when I looked back at the bed
my sleep had messed, betraying me to the knowledge
that we vacate the past by looking on it.

Wasn't that you I saw slumming around there,
enjoying an hour by the pond, watching
the children fold up newspapers into boats and set them afloat?
The water took the tragic newsboats oh so lightly.
A big wind overturned them without looking back
and the geese pulling out from the marges
were leaving their Christmas-tree wakes intact

to ravel outward to possibility or was it
extinction? Yet in spite of everything
afternoons are everything while they are happening
and you are walking home by beef-red houses
drowning in blue sky till the extraordinary moments of dusk—
every night thins to the sucking tide of cars on the street,
a few mysterious sprinklers on manicured lawns,
the canners squeaking down the avenues their
shopping carts burdened like mules with bulging Glad Bags,
about to turn the corner toward whatever will
be the thing they have lost all track of.
Each tomorrow staggers by, like the steps
of the bum tottering giraffelike on two crutches,
a bottle of Thunderbird stuck in his crotch.
He swears at every hermetic car hissing by. But soon
he's a stick figure at the end of a tunnel of oaks,
too small and contemptible to worry over much,
even if part of what tomorrow slurs is true about us.

So the language of the past is too easy a sadness,
whereas we always generalize from within the cool,
spacious, eternal living room of the present.
And though our neighbors are deepened by autumn,
we don't even know what they do there in their windows.
And tomorrow seems entirely indifferent to charity,
so who can blame us if we watch an hour of TV
with the stars unnoticed overhead, raw papery buds
untouched by frost, and car lights swim through ink
and turn the trunks of sycamores into glowworms
and if it happens to be Christmas, archipelagoes of bulbs
celebrate a beautiful innocence, and by spring
the sprinklers turn out their parabolas
while the next century already mists in the trees.
But one day you fall backwards into a night that matters,
kamikaze into an armchair, and all the people
who ever sat there put their arms around you,
the lives that seek you out because you
can't betray them, and while pools of TV blue
make rings around your ankles, on comes

some thirty-second spot about some disaster
on the other side of the world, tonight it's an earthquake,
German shepherds running in and out of the rubble
of a downtown Mexico City hospital, and outside,
in an electronic ear, a boy's faint heartbeat
taps like a blind man's cane for a way out.

For a moment you look up and it's raining so hard
you can't even see the myrtles giving up their blossoms.
Tomorrow is a stone on the other side of the world
you can't move. It is the fact that a little boy
will die, out of the long, bright, slamming, hammering sunlight,
that the volunteers know it, and still they work.
Tomorrow has the one face of our television sets,
which are dumb enough to want to spend their whole
portable existences staring out at whoever
lives behind the other faces, the ones safely concerned,
our dumb, troubling, troubled faces staring into tomorrow.

Vocations

The flies were sleeping on the valleys
of tables, on cold sills,
on windows that couldn't see them,
on ziggurats of books
overdue for weeks,
on the silverish hair of a bum
curled under a palm tree,
dreaming of a better place to sleep
or a worse place.

     *

Once there was a factory
where many people lived.
And once, returning from a refrigerator
with a beer, my father told me
how he'd drawn up the blueprints
for the walls and sweating steel
intestines of another factory.
He had worked in yet another
dirtier, more primitive one
as an adolescent,
and his love for repetition seemed
deadly but not bad.

Industry was in his blood,
a trip each morning
to your endless choice,
long slivers of the mineral hillsides
in the form of butcher knives
the best-paid workers touted at their hips,
his blood was the darker-than-crimson
from the porcine jugular
over his public hands, face, and frock.
His own father, a carpenter,
had nailed the forest
out of attics and hallways.
But he had turned fields of grass into men.

I worked under his roof
and it wasn't hell or anything
an attitude would keep away.
Tonight,
I remember how I got away from it
not for very long
by wondering what they
dreamed of, the older women
of the bacon room that smelled of salt,
steel, and perfume.
The smell of rouge was a kind of wind.
If I dreamed of it now

it would be too vague
to tell apart from the outside world
of sunset-blooded cumulus.
It would be a large cube in the snow
and inside would be snowing,
the conveyor belts lost and separated
from the sound of grinding,
and the foreman would put on pants
of horsehair and bark and miniature bells,
dancing till the workers turned to
curls in the snow, to sleep a million years.
Who'll pay for these imaginings?

                    *

That factory and others,
multiplying in the moonlight,
tamarisk trees brushing the sky,
nowhere wearing through.
Now, during a desert monsoon
lightning in four directions
brings not one drop of water.
But there are frogs on the lawn
glowing like freeways do: nights
when you merge into the displaced traffic
and the green signs there all along
take you back to the childhood you left
in the haste to return.

An old man across the street
licks at his popsicle, and his wife
drops hers with a clumsiness beyond words.
No matter what designs you had for it
the sun has dropped behind the mountains.
I have taken enough harm from people
to believe myself one of them,
to throw my shoes off before sleep,
things dropping from air,
too small to sing like this.

From the Boss Hotel

It might as well keep raining.
The streets might as well be rivers
and taxi drivers, Chinamen poling rafts
across the Yellow River—along the shore
the bums that sleep off that century,
the next. They slink in from history,
I shove my hands through them and cry,
"Get off it, man, you're really drunk."
4:00 A.M. Time to refill bowls with
packets of sugar—the tiny copies
of the famous twentieth-century paintings:
Mirós, Matisse's Fleur-de-Lis or
Chagall's violin player floating off,
held by a blue horse. Art in miniature,
the life emptied out of it, into
the contained black sky of coffee—
a truck driver nudges his buddy,
who's drawn his face, just an oval
burned through with a cigarette.

This evening I passed a dead man
lying in front of a bar. He's no snob,
he lets me talk all day for him:
with each word I speak some of him away
or blow his breath into straws at the
ceiling fans, their glass-blue metal—
pots and pans clanging like Pacific tide
while the whores strut past it all.
Grease sizzles into globes on the grill,
where eggs stare up accusingly.
If I step back from that plateau,
its rising heat, I hear the rain burning
on asphalt; drunks too easy to look at—
the one with his face in his eggs,
lifting his hatched smile from yolk;
who looks at me as if I were a fog

and wincing, thinks he makes out
a friend waving arms, and beyond him
a neon sign, some kind command.

The Only Neighborhood

The night is gone and you suppose you hate it for that.
Morning is also a kind of hate. You step outside
the door and there are no photographs here.
The lackluster streets are not a photograph,
you can't hold that row of houses to the light
where the frame ends and the person begins.

You feel you wouldn't want to be all this,
that looking into yourself the way you do
when you cross the street produces your greed.
That whatever mist seeps through the sidewalk
just slowly enough to soak the trees and lawn
is also you, and you try not to hate that.

And the neighbors who are only your thoughts,
you feel you don't need to talk to them
because they are a part of you, the part
that doesn't want you to hear what you're saying.
The man hosing the dirt from the sidewalk,
the five marbled geese in a child's wading pool,

they and you are not looking out a window.
There's nothing between you and the silly palms
but a lot of time, and still some shadows
behind the stairways, stacked like firewood.
Something burns them one by one, to noon.
What's left gets closer and closer to you.

Trees

Mother passes a bowl
of mashed potatoes.
Outside thirty years ago
it's still storming,
nothing so chaotic
as clouds and potatoes.
Uncle Jense has grains of sand
under his nails from
shingling. The window
frames the trees afraid
because the wind never
stops frightening us.
The house is afraid

without Uncle Jense
nailing its hair down,
afraid we look at it and say,
here are many maples,
elms, the red pines,
whispering about us and
baring their harsh burden
in the harsh treeless air.
Now they are the metaphor
we paint and hide with trees.
Dad says, your grandmother
the night before she died
said not to worry,
there are trees in heaven.

Then I could imagine it,
the tears of resin on
the floors and high roofs.
In the chandeliers' reflection
of the heavenly mansion
we'd stand at the windows,
no better and not much worse
for watching the trees.

Nostalgie du Mal

Goodbye (almost) when night tucked homes away:
there were windows where a single light leaked out

the spirit of the hidden family—windows
like the sockets of the cow's skull my brother

and I put a candle under, switching off
the basement lamps and dancing in that brainless light.

Our shadows on the wall
were divorced from will.

Over the light we passed the map to where it dwarfed our town,
and from a gaping hole tiny flames ran and spread.

Oak Park, Oak Forest, Forest Park, Park Ridge . . .

There Are Many Boats

Miracles instruct or not,
as when the disciples hauled in so many fish
the boat almost sank.
To say more may seem godless,
but I remember pouring a handful of water
as slowly as small hands could,
plashing against the keel of a metal rowboat.
Not far off,
little waves became sound,
metal guy wires clanking metal masts.
The dock burned so slowly
you couldn't see the flames,
those were my father's
scientific words and truly, bobbing,
he held us
in his voice, a sleeve.
Time drifted us out far,
time rocked that all away,
even the quiet that was shutting us out.
I remember other boats,
wherever I was without
thinking about it.
There was a crumpled dollar blowing out
of a friend's hand and almost
across the water.
Later, another,
fainter wind,
black scales on a river,
Manhattan skyline a hardened fire of
leaflessness,
Liberty blinking its oily eye
across our awe.
Another coast,
talking then listening,
I remember a ferry
bringing Vancouver Island, still

another friend telling me in heaven
nights were probably happier than days
and at that same moment
we watched the stern cut a long, wide
tremulous brushstroke
into the makings of a twilit lack of nation. . . .
Our car with others below us, going, like us,
but going nowhere,
the progress that was a miracle of ease,
even the simple
places that came before and after us,
the shore beyond fog,
also took time.

The World's Despite

1941, '42, '43,
the years my mother recurrently dreamt
her father hanged from the oak tree,
swinging by the thread of her dream
while a Japanese bayonet
prodded his stomach, and fear
froze her in hiding behind
the muslin curtain,
kept her from running out to him.
Always she tells her dream in horror,
but always I've pictured it as almost more
honorable to have him there,
swinging in front of his greenhouse—
the thin glass panes steamed opaque,
shielding the flowers winter after winter in
their beautiful living sleep—
he's answering for an elegaic
flower business fertilized by war,
he's swinging over the quiet lawn,
his very body the proverbial
political pendulum;
she's too hypnotized to be alarmed.
The gardener would have to cut him down
before her dream could end,
and from down a long dark hallway
she'd hear a cavernous snoring
and know her father was sleeping,
unharming and unharmed.
1944, the year Aunt Sally
would get herself pregnant
after unzipping her boyfriend's pants
for the incontrovertible reason
he was going to war soon.
I've always pictured her
in the backseat of a Studebaker
down an elm-tunneled street—

streetlights flowering up ahead—
about to undertake her life's one
important decision.
I can't say why I should leave her
having such an impossible time,
but this is always where the picture ends,
out of decency or a censorious
lack of imagination.
That same year, while all Omaha
watched James Cagney and Dennis Morgan,
two Royal Canadian Air Force pilots
in *Captains of the Clouds*,
my flesh-and-blood Uncle Jack
was flying reconnaissance
over a prospering Dresden,
he was eighteen and wetting his pants
inside lilliputian clouds of flak,
the plane spluttering, knocking, but flying
above the global romance.
Next came the year of the bomb,
the party the night before,
when a group of drunken men-children
strewed the Enola Gay
with beer cans and photo-nudes,
women in reclining positions
languishing into the lens,
trying to make the future
come all over them. . . .
I keep straining to think
of the poor Enola Gay
lunging skyward: a mosquito
miles above the earth
blooded with tiny pilots,
the burst protracted under them—
the sky would be inhuman without them.
My mother's dream has passed.
Her hopes have pressed
into a car, a college education,
lipstick, high heels, curled hair,

a husband in a house,
in a succession of houses,
one lovely elm she calls her own
each morning exploding with blackbirds,
those children of the air,
and it's seven years later,
her husband's in the CIC,
he watches his allies the Japanese
beat up Russian spies
on the salt-crusted docks of Osaka.
One day he's walking through the park,
it's necessary to picture the cherry trees
building their bridges of blossom
over his petal-strewn path
and because it's late summer
today he sees an agent friend
gunned down from a bicycle and,
in the parlance of gymnastics,
beautifully executed,
dropping into a cushion
of fallen cherry petals even
newer than the cold war was.
It's always getting dark
in Osaka and Nebraska
when my father ends his story,
and it's already 1959,
my mother pops two more beers
for my father and his brother
and we're all out at sea,
our bulb-lit kitchen table
sailing into a night ridden
by mosquitoes dragging their lean,
bloody, perishable songs
into the untroubled years
between two undeclared wars.
Night would end soon with mother's kiss.
What happened to my uncle's hand? a fist:
I can still remember
the smiles and frowns on each knuckle

coming down like a bomb at
the mere mention of Germans.
I slipped away, slunk down
this stair connecting to that one,
I could hear them from the cellar,
their increasingly drunken-
roaring-airplane voices.
I climbed in a laundry hamper,
fell asleep with various
empty arms and legs tangled around me
and woke to a glowering furnace,
shadows dancing frenzied on the wall,
I mowed them down with a machine-gun broom,
they kept dancing and only I
fell dead, again, again. . . .
Whose sons are the furnace flames?
Whose fathers are the cherry trees?
How short-lived the flames are:
boat lights plying the water
on the other side of memory where
we can't extinguish them,
plying the dark, calling us back
from the unforgivable fire.

II.

Breughel's Peasants and the Month of August

There's too much not to want it all to happen.
The surfeit clothes the summer in daylight wheat,
engulfs the reapers like good weather the short
time it takes for art

to terrorize them into their timeless instant.
Their hopes and fears persist for us unmagnified,
their backs turned on the enormous distances
of the absent God,

the clear reach of the absence of His judgment,
where kids string across meadows at games of luck
and up a cleared furrow a man and woman,
barely two brushstrokes,

beyond the nourishment of consolation,
have just topped the breadcrust hill, with the kingdom
behind them, as if the harvest could happen
with or without them.

Mules in a Field

When Beethoven finished the Fifteenth Quartet
a leaf dropped on the sill,
the air done kissing it.

The notes on the page
settled like birds into an easy sleep
on an autumn evening in Gneixendorf

where his grown-up nephew
finished beating a wool rug,

a cloud of dust slowing down

long before it settles. Carriage dust
sparkling on Bonn's high bay windows.

Beethoven didn't know his nephew was
sorting through his pants pockets
before throwing them over the taboret

and slumping into a sleep

that somehow touches the leaves.
Sleepy, he let his nephew go deeper,

an elbow on the ivory keys.

"Gneixendorf. The name sounds,"

he said out loud,
"like the breaking of an axle-tree."

He couldn't have heard it, or seen
his surprise, face at the window—

mules in a field, openmouthed.
Their braying, unheard, was free,

so he could think how as a child

he was told the forest leaves
fell more quickly moonless nights,

even more so after his father and he
had emptied the forest for home, bed,

falling then, now,
always more easily.

Saint Paul the Hermit, Saint Anthony,

and the Pipistrelles

Paul . . . the first hermit . . . and Anthony,
thinking *he* was the first hermit . . .
—*The Golden Legend*

The cave I have in mind encloses you from the wind-flawed
afternoon light. From a boundlessly patient, gritty desert light.

Paul came here after witnessing a Christian's sacrifice:
the youth, who had his whole body coated with honey,

was then exposed—beneath a blazing sun—to the stings
of flies, hornets, and wasps. Torment, only a pretty flower.

Whereas Paul fled into loneliness. I don't think abnegation
is ever perfect: he carried with him one belonging,

a satchel of sage, and burned his homeland sprig by sprig
to make his cave unholy with the scent and ash.

Sixty years passed. His company, what pipistrelles
returned each spring to flee the mouth and return all night.

This exemplum condenses into a quiet place
with a man in it. This, a few words passing from mouth to mouth,

becomes the rumor that reaches an uneasy Saint Anthony,
another man was lonelier than he was! It took

a centaur, then a satyr, then a wolf to bring
Anthony across a desert to the cave. These are

the two loneliest men on earth, one coming out of the dark,
another out of jealousy: he'd said to Paul

he'd die on the spot rather than go away. The first words
Paul returned were *tell me a story, tell me another,*

there is nothing but pipistrelles to tell of loneliness.
Anthony did, and did; he told of a huge lump of gold

that he shunned on the road to God as if it were fire,
of a silver dish left in a place so remote no man could have lost it.

He told of a saint who sold a penny's worth of sweat
and from the proceeds built a church with only God's blue

face for a ceiling. How the same saint called Death *sister*
and set out honey and the best wines for the winter bees

and made seven little balls of snow, and then before
they could die of the cold, clothed them. *Enough*, Paul said.

Night fell, stars gaped in the cave's mouth, and a crow
brought a loaf of bread neither wanted to bear

the honor of breaking. So they both did, and the bread broke,
a man at each end. Or a saint. A hungry mouth:

they had enslaved themselves to abstinence, which has no end.
But I must tell that as Paul died, Anthony was there

to hold a mirror over the better mouth of the two.
When the circle of steam shrunk to pure reflection,

Anthony could go away. I must tell you neither Anthony
nor Paul's last reflection mourned the death

of the greatest loneliness. Only the pipistrelles,
I must tell you only the stars and the pipistrelles came back

night after night, to chatter all night in the night of night.

In Situ outside Petrograd

Not silence but
silences,
the hills said

to the moon,

speaking back more silences when
most itself,
big old

hole in the cold.

Silences, said the yellow
quills of light
in a stand of larches,

wherein lay a familiar,

a Bolshevik asleep
inside a horse still
warmly unalive.

The next day,

long live the next day,
the moist silence of the fumes
of his breath.

Withheld from him now.

The road baring his frozen tracks
across itself
follows the river where in spring

not now

barges pull coal
beyond their wakes,
beyond the waves breaking,

the waves breaking quietly apart.

Addressing His Deaf Wife, Kansas, 1908

The clear obsession that holds up the walls
and rafters of sunlight and pulls everything down
isn't what holds my talk together.
I touch and you touch. Just
who am I talking to? Explorers
made names on lies,
there used to be passenger pigeons in numbers
far beyond understanding
but the stories outsized the flocks:
fur traders said the Mandan tribes kept
unthinkably huge pots of the pigeon oil
boiling gray at both sides of a village.
Remember how once in anger you dipped my hand
in a vat of boiling red dye?
When I screamed to have you hear my pain
I had committed a lie
of intention, and the lie, like love,
was larger than either you or me.

Sometimes I'll tell you stories
to have you watch me listen. For instance:
I should be walking outside,
awhile on the dirt road that leads to town.
Standing alone, with you at the window;
the clouds now dragging curtains of rain
across the great Midwest,
which holds to very little.
Yes, the grass matters: even in rain
the hills bursting from their seams.
For you the wind among the apple trees
is more dynamic for its unheard strengths,
unquestionable as my sitting up just now.
I'm terrified both by what
I do and what I don't do, and terror,
like anything human and said,
survives just beyond understanding.

Mr. and Mrs. Samuel McCall

The nineteenth century half over,
she stands there looking out
at the approaching storm blackening the hills
and the children who ignore it, who jump
from the porch like packages of light.
She has been washing her hair. It drips
on the tessellated floor.
When she swings it back around her
like an heirloom fur, it throws
warm water through his ghost, on the window—
where the voices of her young children
break and never reach them.

He looks just as he did before
the wedding, years younger. She wants
to tell him how thinking back always
makes her alone, even if children
sometimes hang from her yellow muslin dress
like a cluster of grapes. Is he still warmed
by the same frustration he felt
the time she took a milkweed pod
and threw it at the beveled mirror;
seed-shadow across the mirror, across them both—

maybe he still feels it, how this yard,
wild or not, seems worth knowing,
the blackened branches ending in gray squirrels,
one leaf that falls down
like a waving hand. Maybe he sees himself
growing through these things, ravaged
by his children playing maypole, casting up
leaves like the clouds now shredding
through the Norway spruce so odd here in Virginia.
How slowly they took shape, his children,
still solid, blown among myrtle.

The Hand of God and a Few Bright Flowers

Probably the hotel yard is still choked with hydrangeas,
their blue heads bobbing, bowing harshly, living under the wind. Probably
the same stale sufferings are visible, businessmen holding their bowlers
to their skulls, dogs wrenching their legs awkwardly
to piss—but new dogs, new cloaks, new bowlers. A pot of basil
now rests in the window niche where Rodin hid, to take in
each reception for the poet Victor Hugo, each last entertaining smile and
twitch of the poet. Reeling off hundreds of studies,
one by one Rodin stripped away the washed-out countenances
like the thin, translucent skin of a cellar onion
just before it spoils for good—it's a wonder
anything was left when Rodin was finished with the man.

If I had been born a cow just off to the side of the road
to Meudon, one January I would have seen
a crate shimmying almost free from the ropes
tying it to a wobbly carriage. With every bump, the poor crate jumped
as if the statue wanted out and even the stone that suffered
the soft-edged figure of the incomparable poet
would have liked him to raise a hand with the majestic sweep,
the significance of rural ocean outstretching
its folds of blue-white January snow with farms
lost in it . . . the carriage driver has taken five drams
of laudanum to calm his nerves,
has just passed a plane tree in that last leafless degree
of remove—he thinks it looks like a hand.
If I could touch his back

I would feel it clench like a fist. Each lamplike tendon
would seem to glow with the complete man—looking at his back

would be stepping from some wide and windy space
into a museum filled with visitors: everything is crowded
and dark: there's no curator here to explain
the sculptures and paintings,
only sculptures with rigid, inimical gestures,

only paintings cracking to explain themselves and why
they face each other off in the crowded halls.

Rodin had placed all the sketches of the great poet
in the bright din of noon refracted by all the village
doors, windows, cubbies, passersby, lingerers, kids torturing kids.
Hundreds of Victor Hugos looked out of that light,
came at Rodin like women leaning out of their windows

to take in the first signs of weekday life: a street cleaner
stamping at the gutter water to clean his muddy boots
even though his soul, like the filthy sweater
on his back, was by now barely even a moth-eaten scrim—
just by looking at him the serious women could tell
he was the kind of sod on which all pity,
all contempt is lost—because if you wronged him by crossing
the path of his broom or placing a fat, sweaty penny
in his palm, he'd stare at you, unperplexed
from behind a deep satisfaction, knowing charity is hatred,
while the twilight stares out from behind the cedars:

and there in the middle distance

a concourse of business and activity, pretty flowers and
children and businessmen walking abruptly, crisp with their own attention
to themselves—which is how it should be: a village
mysteriously aloof in its parts, its run of faces dismissing every twitch
the twilight tears loose. The windows close. The street cleaner goes as they
all go off to the side. One workhorse
drilling a clumsy, steaming signature in the snow:

it's a wonder the village survived the sculpture of Victor Hugo.

No, it's a wonder my cat hasn't yet disturbed my papers
or I might have wrung its . . . no,
the cat is entangled in a ball of yarn. The cat's
obsession is dreaming the cat, and as it unravels, it
becomes stronger until undone into a hopelessly fabulistic
remnant of an obsession: like water

pouring from the glass back into the pitcher,
the cat pours into my lap. What a day already—
its closed eyes making frowns like the mouths of reeled-in trout.
The cat would have stayed with me, except that motion,
like water, clearly gives over to more, like water slung off a

wheel.

On the road to Meudon that January
the carriage driver had decided that calm was not enough.
Five drams later, he was nodding with a vision:
his two healthy hands have been pollarded
for no good reason, and with the gusto of the healthy elms they are,
they have begun to sprout leaflets. They do this to the trees
in his neighborhood in the summer so that in winter
the snow-sleeved branches don't cave in on the roofs.
The driver, staring at his summer elms,
somehow still gripping the reins,
wonders how snow can fall. Always snow—
the crate with the statue of Victor Hugo takes another
turn of his vision slowly tapering off to
a dim red bowler ringing the farmland. Dusk trapped in the white

empires of laudanum. The Hotel Lusignan, where
Victor Hugo entertained and Rodin hid out of respect
and hoping not to tamper with his inspiration,

for all I know may be
closed down. The hand that once hewed
the hand of God is dust now,
certainly we can count on that. The carriage,
the carriage driver, the street cleaner,
the obsession of my cat shall all be dust falling to what dust
builds to. But Hugo's onion-domed Moscow shall survive Napoleon
and his men, who hid in the bellies of dead horses. Meudon, Paris,
Berlin, Moscow, the Hotel Lusignan haven't yet been
returned to the chaos—out of which the hand of God
still grasps, unloosing a man and a woman
kicking their way out of an unhewn fragment of marble—

welter of arms and legs. Let's say the hand of God
can't release the man and woman because
this original reach can create but it can't destroy.
Then man and woman are like the pair of sycamores
in the yard across my street—they seem to fountain
out of the sleeves of their mouldering bark
into the bare air in which they face each other, their branches
are summer, are a noon-bright so white
it seems all seeing. I would have to give
Rodin and God the benefit of the doubt
and say that even if God's reach by now can destroy,
only man destroys outward in,
hewing away at marble with nothing less than violence,

to say nothing of tenderness.

To Darwin Reading the Bible

Say forgiveness is a white hand, yours,
turning a page—Noah and wife rocking to the same
sad song. She leans back, eyes reflecting seven
different finches, puma bristling, mosquitoes,
and those ghosts of neighbors she thinks she sees
behind her closed eyes. You see your mind
behind the shoreline cedars, those outstretched limbs.

The mind is outlined by a walk to the window.
Your mind, their mind, it didn't have a name
for those miles-long stripes of "dark-yellowish
or mudlike water" that parted for you, the messenger.
And now dusk asks your forgiveness. A white hand
turns a page under kerosene. The cuttlefish
glows, a surrogate lamp. Dusk has waited for you

to ask your forgiveness. The atrocious food,
fields of confervae the sailors call sea-sawdust,
the captain's hysteria and his lisp, are constants,
musical frogs, part of the crescent the sea and sky
make. The crescent behind each day you shore and always
you take your mother and father into the trees
with you. If one can forget the weight of going,

and be the judge of anything but his own happiness,
he can say, assuredly—the day began with cuttlefish,
dusk is a book whose thinning pages you can turn
but can't leave a marker. When the window quavers,
so does its landscape. And in the end the skull
and the boat are sorry they couldn't be larger,
are sorry what you received was only beginning.

The Leeches

Back then the leeches sucked the blood of dying men and women
through long brass tubes, or if the leech were a poor one,

through bulrush reeds plucked from the brows of bogs.
Though sickness was unnatural, the cure was always natural:

if a woman couldn't nourish a child, they gave her the milk
of a cow of one color, and she spewed it into a stream;

they took a piece of her last child's grave, wrapped it in black wool
and sold her sorrow for her; and she went into another

house than that she went out from, and ate, and drank.
Or for those who couldn't see from sunset to sunrise,

so when the broadness of the earth came between them and the sun
and cast a night silvered with the rough stubble of the stars,

they couldn't see the hand hoisting bread and murder to the mouth,
for those, the leeches toasted the kneecap of a buck, squeezed

the ooze from a turd, to smear the eyes therewith, and it
was soon better for them—just let the dusk come crying,

for then no weeds but wouldn't be turned to herbs,
mugwort, waybroad facing the morning sun, sinfull, feverfew,

old soap, slime of water and ash; then no charm but wouldn't be sung
against thorn blister, against ice blister, worm blister,

against the breath of the worm carried in the wind,
against the North Wind rattling open the North Gate each time

winter made its admonishing fanfare in the cemetery.
Until one day threats crossed the water intact, and Byrhtnoth

and the dear gray shapes who loved him crumpled to the ground
and the dawn uncovered no cure, only a few groves

bearing ruby berries not even the starving deer ate.
The sucking surf cried with gannets and seamews

and one by one they took seaward—bright specks, then
invisible in the first iodine tinctures—and once again

winter had brought too much snow and too much consequence.
Thus the leech of Essex found his friend and kin and earl

and taking cinquefoil, daisy, and red nettle, and working them
into a dust and mixing them with a stream of virgin honey

snipped into two with a knife, he poured the mixture
from an eggshell into the sockets. With the eyes missing,

two golden lakes appeared: he sang a charm as well
as could be sung into that red smear of a mouth:

the salt sea must disperse, the very stars must be snuffed
when I the venom from you blow. An undulating V

of geese carried their bleary consonant southward,
a feather switchbacked onto a now breathless mouth,

another feather turned in one of the lakes. The leech stood
over him like the whole world taking a last look, and left.

Now dwarf dostle, wild cucumber, and colewort stalk go unpicked
and patients enchanted as the flowers sit in waiting rooms,

while into the hospitals the moon stares blankly as a doctor
when he cauterizes a wound with a dab of silver nitrate.

But back then, to fail at healing was to be as small as death asked,
for sooner or later the leeches, too, were smashed, drowned, or they

simply collapsed in time—call it running water—done
clinging to rock face to escape the currents and thus the water

veined through this earth toward the mickle ocean
and neither ocean nor river had any place but on earth.

III.

Mockingbirds

I found a pool of feathers today
in the front yard. Some of them were
the gray of low clouds gliding in
from Mexico, others the color of rust
on the lip of the water tap
that sulks above the burnt foxtail,
others whiter than silk or ghost breath.
There was a blurred silence between colors.
If it had left the privilege
of prismatic chaos, the silences
between cries, how had its soul
entered my wonder, a houselight
left on by someone on a long trip?

They have what the dead only become,
a dragging fender, cat-shrill, leaves
paving the air red. Whitman
thought the mockingbird contained all birds,
so when one fell, an entire phylum
gave way to the stupified fact.
A dismantled headdress, scattering.
Up to the trees they trail a blue
as uncertain as a propane flame, reciting
what they feel at what they hear.

Looking in my window now—a few
cacti, a jade cockroach, unmailed letters—
I find my life without me strange,
unmoved by my absence. One tilted lampshade.
For now bravery means staying inside
a place or a thought for more than
protection, just as the bird dips
indifferently to shadow rising in the pond,
lost in the brain it hasn't mastered.
I can't tell which birds in my dreams
have long been dead, savagely lighting on
the branch just outside the window,
until I wake, until I release them.

In Memory of Jean Rhys

her father's telescope

The Carib stillness sundered by the mail,
the Royal Steamer, shabbiest of the lot.
And other steamers. Triangles taking sail.
A hull-less fishing boat, its cargo of rot—
all circumscribed by blackness, like that cloud
that never cleared, with strangers on the deck
rushing to seats before cloud shadow shrouds
them and the memory of them, the deck.
Childhood reduced to just those things you hold
in a father's enormous brass telescope,
the mail for others pouring through the cold,
nicked eyepiece. Hummingbirds, hibiscus, the tropes
of shoreside mimes became that part of you
you'd never touch, a bright jungle that grew.

2
Dominica

The thinned-out tide of dawn recoils
from shores that drain, sizzle like fat,
from bones where every landing gnat
has eyes like tourists' on the spoils.

Each grain of sand, small and still.
Nearby you in a pool of gray,
a shirt whose man dissolved away.
A seagull's shadow plows the swill.

You step on something. Water squirts;
a bulb of kelp bursts like a brain.
Far down the beach two walkers wane
to specks. Just looking at them hurts.

A rotting cedar lifts a hand
to ships that climb the ocean's wall
with all the speed of snails, and crawl
over the edge, cut off from land.

3
"Bertha"

Outside the window
sparrows the tree holds
in its grip on the world, taking
everything it can.

Outside your mind, a network
of forgotten streets and dates,
the never-encountered: skaters
pirouetting on last year's pond

with your love of snow were snow,
were the way the white room opened
into the larger room of trees and
endlessly snowing walls and ceilings.

4
Point Lobos

A Christmas sun, no brighter than any sun
that reappears between clouds, and is gone.
It had left that it might return, reveal
this moment to us, strapped behind the wheel,
burning to walk on earth. 1979, we get out.
The stepping worries my parents. Mother's out
of father's sight, who's not sure why we stopped.
By her side all these years, now he's scared.
He feels he's in a novel, whoever
reads it too hungover to turn the page
that has him walking from his frightened son.

The idea that the cypress should die off
not because of man but simply because
their destiny was to make this last grotesque stand
might well have been a novelist's idea.
Only the story knows who is happy.
And I can't help my parents when they fight
or Jean Rhys whose life made her miserable.
All types outstripped, as where waves crash
and gulls and terns dip hard to outlast wind
but barely move against it. All this work
to hear the sea lions, make out heads or tails.
Three hundred yards out, they're blobs that wiggle.
Just how their skin endures the water scares
us, who will never know: such clarity
will make some miserable, others happy.

The Dead Monkey

A face framed in a pink lace baby's hood was youth and age
collapsed to a wizened black walnut. It had no idea
that we were there, New Orleans, 1981, or that we were
growing envious of its owner, an unshaven but rich-looking Mexican
who hoisted it from the ground, not altogether modest
about the attention he and it were getting from all of us,
eating our beignets, watching this binary configuration,
man and monkey, kiss, kiss again, patching up
some make-believe quarrel between lovers.
Suddenly it leapt up a trellis of morning glory vines,
swung from a brass chandelier over the human circus of breakfasters
and scrambled across the street into a moving bus,
arms and legs toppling one over the other
as it tried to keep up with its death.
The man walked out to the ridiculous end to his happiness,
stealing the delight from us, like surreptitious newlyweds,
poor enough in spirit to be amazed by fact.
Taking it in his arms, crying to make himself alone,
this Mexican was living proof that suffering
is not all that crazy about company.
When the crowd dispersed, he seemed relieved,
as if too much had already been suffered
without us adding our thimbleful.
That night we saw the Mexican without his monkey in a bar,
buying everyone drinks and laughing hysterically
about the whole thing, saying *death is my life*.
If that sounds a bit dramatic, blame it
on sweet bourbon, this is just what he said,
being just lucid enough to mix up life and death
and stupid enough to want to share in their confusion.
We toasted with him to stupidity because
there's not always enough stupidity around to celebrate,
and when we were good and drunk we turned ourselves out into the night,
between more bars we saw more bars,
windows like photographs fleshed out with

bodies that destroyed their secrets,
we took the journey across the dangerous street,
entranced by the idea of getting somewhere,
sick for everything but home.

Over and Under the Sun

You slept, I watched the pilot
arc us around an anvil
that would have killed us all.
The way he said it
was *going around the weather.*
The fierce marble profile tiara-ed
with sun-spokes was
more brilliant from
outside and more dangerous
than the wide, undivided brim
of the horizon

is imaginable or possible.
I read: *To the Lighthouse,*
turning from the heavens
to a woman who watched a schooner
sink below, then reemerge
on the horizon with her
unsavable friends and
their helpless shame:

other books turned over as
silent as rooftops.
Seeming to move
without moving is the worst
of the heaviness. . . .

       ✻

Whether censorship mothers
symbol or not,
before the dark
age ends, I swear
it's what falls off from us
that interests most,
so tonight, nearly
the emptiest night ever to feel

so empty of myself
I get up, leave her
on the square blossom
of our bed, and wash
the sweat from the
face in the mirror,
and the harm there turns away,
forever untouched.

The wind looks into
itself and changes,
still clicking leaves
against our windows,
the way the careless TV blur
changes on her flesh—
she's dreaming of light—
nothing but her past
out there, before her.
Who it is she loves
wants more than heaven or
a woman behind him, asleep

and nearly dead,
letting him look at her like this,
this abandon more intimate than sex.

*

Sun gets swallowed by tamarisks
like clouds, by clouds
amorphous beyond likeness.
Of course, it's always getting
into earthbound trouble,
this whale-back hill
breaching, burying it for good,
jets like days peopled
with tiny abstractions
rubbing it out an instant.
Too long it goes, and yet
in its stored warmth we can talk
about next to everything,

hope that everything
scares us alive when it's gone.
That, and as we cut
across the schoolyard
on an old or new way home,
the last shade of eucalyptus
on our eyes,

say the sun had small intentions
like the moisture that gleamed
cold days on car windows.
Too gone to see, yet it
colors the cold, violent
voices of serious children,
voices crossing the blacktop
minus their names. Take, love,
my own name, Bill, meaning
all the debits and credits
too gone to know, all the times
you spoke it, sometimes angrily,
sometimes like a stringless kite
past the high wires of conversation,
up there in a clean blue place,
a gap in the background of all
we have to turn to besides ourselves.

Envy

Hours, seasons of it. Instants when I'm
always very nearly about success.

Espaliered bushes climb and conclude
the ladders they are of sun and moist black soil

and we see night by day. The sun climbing,
climbing down a break in the clouds too slow in healing to heal

our rich, poor, black-mother-of-pearl shadows.
Columns, porticoes

to slash the sun into shade to look out from.
From inconsequence. From being judged

for the sway I have over a few. From a trash can
nearby, someone's foot comes up, a voiceless scuff,

footsteps hardly audible at first, and then too far to wish away.
It's hunger that makes a sound like that—

it's tracing, untracing each thought friendly or not,
each passerby's strange, facial moonscape

every afternoon. Shadows filling with heat.
Wanting to be the kind of light after fog clears

and the trees and whatsoever they shade are still there,
the parti-colored joggers,

neighbors telling their dog to go to hell,
the words not doing it,

mockingbirds whittling day away always always.
How survivable

the self is,
wondering after fanfare,

looking out a screen door torn from its hinges,
its coming and going forsaken—

past palms that shake their rastafarian heads,
never thinking to get in the way,

deferring, deferring.
Only the endless could never be jealous.

December

While sirens shriek through the urban hum of a balmy November,
I'd like to take a stab at the life of young Chaucer,
and place him under a brawny, oaken table,
between his merchant-class father's legs. *You have to lie*
to get at the truth is a lie. And lying kills,
sometimes. Applause for the ashen, rag-sheathed peasant
tending the fire, sluggishly turning cold hands over it.
Forgive his standing off from royalty. Forget him because
the Black Prince, toasting, just dropped his glass of wine;
it makes a crimson lake on the table lined with watercress
to resemble the meadows and rills where kings hunt. Troops
outside the castle pack in as tight as grains of wood
around the patient profiteers dealing looted bread
and inside, the pregnant silences of the prince
must be abided by the lesser tipplers. Does their dim,
dumb look come from behind the glaze of patience or
submission? Snow from under the door makes a little pile.
Outside my window, adolescents pile into cars, squeal off.
At the end of an otherwise normal day a broken fire hydrant
gives up a ribbon of water. At the end of a week
water goes on fraying as a cause without beginning.
In Jefferson High School the students have made Möbius strips,
cutting each one lengthwise, to end up with one strip
twice as long as the first one. The moral: geometry
tells us we go home richer for having incised
our ends down the middle, but history tells us we
go away—before anyone knows our seats have emptied.

By night each headlight alters the fraying ribbon.
By morning I'm awake; by noon morning was a faint
remembering. It's actually hot today. Tomorrow
I'll find a Möbius strip in a puddle of water, connecting
as well as ever, and one more day will toe the line.
The young Chaucer will have crawled out from the table
to see—by the sooty athletics of the fire jugglers
at both ends of the table—two miniature castles of wattled hay

translate into fire. Ashes catch on merchant-class lips
like the ragged crows that light on the manned crenellations.
Soon it will be the beginning of another December.
Tires squealing, an entire city in heat, cars on cinder blocks
at the ends of the farthest alleys. By night
fog bandages the skyline, and the hot-pink Sears sign
floats disconnected from enterprise, and by morning
the kids have twisted their mouths into tough smiles
and piled back into their high school, slumbering
the heroic sleep of boredom and disapproval.
Night spliced into day approves us as long as we prove
patient, but I'm afraid that patience can outlast
the virtue of patience. Outside the castle it's snowing.
Inside, Chaucer tries to, but can't imagine the mud-dark road
running wildly between the snow-bright fields, toward home.
And the child who lives more may not have lived
more clearly than his father or his father's uncle,
both of whom, long ago, the Were River almost froze.

Five Years

Side by side she and I ate our picnic lunches
and wondered which of our gestures we'd give up
as useless, borrowed, not our parents' to release.
A woman across the street hanged whites that flapped
trying to wake decisively but getting nowhere.
Her husband stooped to the watermelons, blimps
too heavy with seed and flesh to glide over housetops.
These his work, we liked watching him hover there,
wind fraying the hose-water, a mud-blossom on his brow,
something always about to happen, as in paintings,
pauses; and we brooded over the shared perception
like night above a lamp, for daytime was nighttime
or something finer than nighttime, as a shadow
behind falling water is only in spirit a shadow,
the untouchable adumbration of some fullness.

Waking now by a lake in northern Wisconsin
I grasp at the sound of branches rubbing shingles
and entering a life, too much to hate or fear.
I see a man in a rented rowboat, plumbing for depths.
The swallows can't help us. I enjoy watching them.
I remember their form without their precise motions,
which I feel I have somehow given up in advance,
while a man rowing toward shore steps from his boat
unencumbered by the bottoms he failed to reach.
In time you extricate yourself from love and loss
but then, in a yellowed diary, waking under the trees
somewhere back there you find yourself writing.
You've forgotten just who was behind it all,
who the crossed-out words were supposed to protect,
who could have known what would still frighten.

Water

Through Bridge City the bus's roof
whisked the lower limbs of oaks,
a scraping behind our sleep
and insomniacal talk.
The weak cones of reading light
dimmed each time the driver braked,
and when we all arced over the bridge
faces looked up from newspapers—down
to a barge-lit river and a row of houses
on a gimpy leg of sea water.
Sailboats, yachts, houseboats nearly
lapped across a highway our highway
passed over. Upon which sight went
everywhere, past travel and sleep
into the swamps where there were docks
without a shore. Here I was. Here,
sleeping, you were silent
and your silence had a closed mouth;
you were holding a sunflower
with a face, all seed once,
like the eyes of the mosquitoes
drawing down the silhouettes
of nighthawks, starlings, and swifts.
The flower was a ransacked eye!
and everything that could be said
about what was, what is, and what will be.
Of how six hours through rain on pilings
our grand slumming in New Orleans had thinned
to a memory of two cranes
above new buildings, a single crane
in a boatyard, water
half swallowing a no-litter sign,
transparent advice of water
breaking but not really breaking.
Your sleeping hand had forgotten
it was holding a dead flower.

The flower might as well have been
a memory. I took up space
and watched the way you took up space.
At the end of each tiny road
refineries burned, so remote from day
they looked like settings to movies
about a purely aesthetic future.
Two days surrounded every night;
two eyes closed down every face.
The bus stopping for some obscure
reason only the driver knew,
the few who woke bustled, a voice
at the end of a silence. You
woke, we talked, before you fell back
asleep with your flower, whose dead
face jerked when the bus jerked
farther than ever between two days,
where I would sleep and let rain fall
for all I care and all I care for.

Eighteen Species of Hummingbirds

I hurry to find the name in the bird book, but
like what we are all dying to call reality,
the bird's gone when I come back.
The book closed, three more appear all lacking names—like
rufous, blue-throated, black-chinned, Anna's, Allen's—
the best part of me trembles to see the small and jeweled
suspended above the blood-red, broken-fisted
blossoms of the flagellant ocotillo.
They're perched upon nonexistent twigs,
bills thrust out from emerald haloes of wings,
even the changing remove they keep from each other
being beautiful, and with the thorned
tentacles swaying in the same remove,
the same bare air, the only place they meet,
I wish my body could bloom for them.
                                         One night
I dreamt of hummingbirds: I was on some
inscrutable mission as usual,
with a domestic end, which led me to
the kitchen, opening all the cupboards—
a hummingbird had made a nest under
the sink, in the plumbing, which dripped honey
instead of water—into a coffee can
there for that purpose: to collect the surfeit
the hummingbird didn't need—and there in the nest
stitched from carpet, lint, shirt threads, and spider webs
two fledglings, sherbet-bright bugs, were hatching
out of the same nowhere, the same necessity
from which the mother appeared, the reading of my wish,
and as the overseer of delicacy
she pumped food into their stomachs with a jabbing
that looked like the murder of the innocents.

What of her painstaking skills, her nurturing
the purely helpless and gawking—had my dream wished her
nearly into a murderer, was murder

what I wanted, and what house was this my
dream erected? I woke outside houses
altogether, camped above Tucson, under a pine
up among crimson tatters—and looked up
to an entire meadow living under
who'd believe it maybe a hundred hummingbirds
sucking from whippled beardtongue and phlox—I must
have wished myself here. They hovered from one blossom
down to another, which stood below, open.
I was inside their sky, they must have seemed
too weak to walk on ground for me to wish them luck,
the honeyed, the nervous, up to their necks in blossom.

Public Gardens

As if all day the Milky Way came down
to shrub rows and hillocks of raked weed, we study

the fog to exercise our part in it.
The largeness that's everywhere is us

nowhere we stand, and when fog lifts
no romantic stars or starlets are coupling

in that empty copse, love. We
stand there and watch how pretty the nothing is,

and our shadows cross the husk of a watch
stuck at 2:30. Each moment dies twice,

once for itself, once for the love of it,
once in moonlight, once so the sun can shine

over who- or whatever lived out their flaws
and slower perfections. We stand and talk

so our shadows can pretend to stand and talk.
Could they ever want to hear how briefly

orange blossoms settled when a whirlwind collapsed?
Could the flatness of their grounded gestures

inhabit the roses named by dying dowagers—
Snow over Chicago, Storybook,

Sunrise Sunset, Babbling Brook, and *Vanity*—
names that gloss over a dying plot.

A square in the past. A handkerchief blowing
through night's lunar silences,

embroidered with twigs, pollen, and birds
whose empty bones must give them horrible dreams.

There's more hollowness, *Heavenly Bamboo*
from China and Japan, lovingly shaded

by the *Marsh Grapefruit*, West Indies.
We're demure sometimes in places like this

because they're everything we can't express.
As if those boughs were the hands of a lover,

two lovers, many lovers, all their branching hands
in moonlight playing over flesh.

Whether our own gnawing is that diffuse,
it took the plants of every continent,

spring and autumn dancing hand in hand,
to compose paradise, when it scattered

with the mistake and some bad weather.
It comes back sometimes, a

moment when a breeze in autumn
seems springlike, or when a hinge squeaks,

a thin sound, like winter,
behind everything. But just one moment

he wanted her to leave his side,
leave behind their bower for sleep

and anything that brought them closer,
just try to bear what little would be left.

Notes

"Saint Paul the Hermit, Saint Anthony, and the Pipistrelles"—
a corruption of the lives of these two saints as told in *The Golden Legend*.

"Addressing His Deaf Wife, Kansas, 1908"—the first two lines are
adapted from a poem by Richard Pevear.

"Mr. and Mrs. Samuel McCall"—the source is a collection of "true"
ghost stories, the author of which I cannot remember.

"The Leeches"—a few phrases come from *Leechdoms, Wortcunning,
and Starcraft of Early England*, translated by Oswald Cockayne.

"To Darwin Reading the Bible"—the quotes are from *Voyage of the
Beagle*.

"Public Gardens"—the one I have in mind is the Tucson Botanical
Gardens. Milton writes line 37 about paradise.

I would like to thank Richard Lyons, Susan Prospere, and David
Wojahn for all their help and encouragement.

Poetry from Illinois

History Is Your Own Heartbeat
Michael S. Harper (1971)

The Foreclosure
Richard Emil Braun (1972)

The Scrawny Sonnets and
Other Narratives
Robert Bagg (1973)

The Creation Frame
Phyllis Thompson (1973)

To All Appearances: Poems New
and Selected
Josephine Miles (1974)

The Black Hawk Songs
Michael Borich (1975)

Nightmare Begins Responsibility
Michael S. Harper (1975)

The Wichita Poems
Michael Van Walleghen (1975)

Images of Kin: New and
Selected Poems
Michael S. Harper (1977)

Poems of the Two Worlds
Frederick Morgan (1977)

Cumberland Station
Dave Smith (1977)

Tracking
Virginia R. Terris (1977)

Riversongs
Michael Anania (1978)

On Earth as It Is
Dan Masterson (1978)

Coming to Terms
Josephine Miles (1979)

Death Mother and
Other Poems
Frederick Morgan (1979)

Goshawk, Antelope
Dave Smith (1979)

Local Men
James Whitehead (1979)

Searching the Drowned Man
Sydney Lea (1980)

With Akhmatova at the Black Gates
Stephen Berg (1981)

Dream Flights
Dave Smith (1981)

More Trouble with the Obvious
Michael Van Walleghen (1981)

The American Book of the Dead
Jim Barnes (1982)

The Floating Candles
Sydney Lea (1982)

Northbook
Frederick Morgan (1982)

Collected Poems, 1930–83
Josephine Miles (1983)

The River Painter
Emily Grosholz (1984)

Healing Song for the Inner Ear
Michael S. Harper (1984)

The Passion of the Right-Angled Man
T. R. Hummer (1984)

Dear John, Dear Coltrane
Michael S. Harper (1985)

Poems from the Sangamon
John Knoepfle (1985)

Eroding Witness
Nathaniel Mackey (1985)
National Poetry Series

In It
Stephen Berg (1986)

Palladium
Alice Fulton (1986)
National Poetry Series

The Ghosts of Who We Were
Phyllis Thompson (1986)

Moon in a Mason Jar
Robert Wrigley (1986)

Lower-Class Heresy
T. R. Hummer (1987)

Poems: New and Selected
Frederick Morgan (1987)

Cities in Motion
Sylvia Moss (1987)
National Poetry Series

Furnace Harbor: A Rhapsody
of the North Country
Philip D. Church (1988)

The Hand of God
and a Few Bright Flowers
William Olsen (1988)
National Poetry Series

Bad Girl, with Hawk
Nance Van Winckel (1988)

She is stunningly beautiful, and she will never age, Grace thought. *Ten years from now, or twenty or thirty, when the years weigh down upon me, she will still be young and beautiful in this portrait—and in Alistair's memory.*

At first glance the painting seemed calm and serene; but despite the slight smile on those sweetly painted lips, there was something wrong, something deeply unsettling about Finnula's portrait. She stepped closer.

It is the shadows, Grace realized. At first it had appeared to her that Finnula was stepping out of the darkness. Now she had the impression that it was the reverse, that the shadows were enfolding Finnula into the blackness. Absorbing her.

Although her feet stayed planted on the ground, Grace felt as if she were being pulled, gently but inexorably, out of her body and into the painted scene. A wave of fragrance enveloped her: rose geranium, lavender, and bergamot . . .

. . . Her entire world had been distilled into this single moment: moonlight glazing the ancient stones like hoarfrost, the night air filled with the poignancy of summer's ripe scents fading into smoky autumn.

Regret welled up inside her along with a terrible longing . . . a primal ache for things that never were—and now would never be . . .

"Is something wrong, madam? Are you taken ill?"

Grace blinked at the sound of the butler's voice. For a moment she didn't know where she was. *Who* she was.

"Madam?" Braedon touched her arm and she was instantly jerked back into the present, as if her soul had been stretched to the limits of its tether, then snapped back inside her body like a band of India rubber. Her pulses hammered and her insides vibrated with the recoil.

She shook her head to clear it. "I was just . . . just admiring the portrait."

Braedon's face was carefully blank. "Which portrait would that be, madam?"

Grace turned back and felt the blood drain from her face. There was no painting there at all: only a darker rectangle of burgundy silk to show where one had been recently removed.

Chapter Sixteen

Grace gathered her wits and her courage. "I should say, rather, that I had come to admire the portrait of the first Mrs. McLean that was hung here. What have you done with it?"

Braedon blinked. "Mr. McLean asked me to remove it to the music room and put another in its place."

"To spare my feelings, no doubt." She took a deep breath and issued her first order as mistress of the house. "It was kindly meant, but I am sure it would cause Miss Janet grief to find her mother's portrait gone. Please replace it, Braedon. If my husband should inquire, you will tell him that I directed you to do so."

His faint smile was the only hint of his approval. "As you wish, madam."

"Have you seen my stepdaughter this morning?"

"Yes, madam. Miss Janet has gone to the solar, as she does every morning after breakfast."

Following Braedon's directions, Grace cut across the terrace to the courtyard formed by the three wings of the house. The medieval section was in the center, linking the old with the new. The old casement windows reflected a blue and cloudless sky. The September sun was warm on her face as she crossed the flagstoned court, but Grace felt chilled.

She glanced over at the ancient tower off to her left. At its foot the loch gleamed like a mirror of dark blue glass, until a fish leaped up, shattering it into ever-expanding circles of shimmering silver light. The green hills on the opposite shore stood out sharply against the misted mountains in the distance.

Finnulla always loved this view, Grace thought. She was instantly aghast. Where had it come from, this strange knowledge that had embedded itself in her mind, as if the memory of it were her own?

This sudden and startling connection to Finnula frightened her.

She hesitated outside the oak door to the medieval wing, wondering if it was wise to enter. A terrible sense of dread clung to her, wrapped itself around her like a shroud. Glancing back the way she'd come, she saw Braedon hovering by the open drawing room windows. *I must not let him know that anything is wrong!*

She opened the door and stepped inside. Her brain was alert, her nerves on edge as she let the aura of the place fill her. Nothing occurred to disturb her. The only scents were beeswax polish and wood and a faint touch of something exotic she couldn't name. She sighed in relief. *It is just a lovely old hall in the morning sun.*

The heavy door swung shut behind her. It was a large room, with high windows on both sides, and a fine hammerbeam ceiling. The stone chimney breast above the enormous hearth was carved with the McLean coat of arms and flanked by two standing candelabra filled with fat candles. She could see that it would make a fine ballroom for the masquerade that Alistair had told her would be held during the coming house party.

Taking the stairs to the next floor, she found the solar at the top, just as the butler had described it. The door stood open. Janet was sitting at a narrow table, building a house from a deck of cards. She didn't look up when Grace entered. Tongue between her even white teeth, she took the last card and carefully placed it to roof in the third level of the pasteboard structure. It wobbled, but held.

Janet lifted her head and smiled at Grace. "There! I did it!"

For a moment she looked happy and very young. Then her pretty features twisted. With a sudden sweep of her arm, she brushed the cards aside. The little house collapsed in a heap; but one card went spinning across the ancient boards to land at Grace's feet.

She stooped down and picked it up. "The ace of spades," she commented, returning it to the table.

"The death card," Janet said, with a good deal of solemn pleasure.

There, Grace thought, *the gauntlet has been laid down.* She smiled back at the girl. "If you are trying to frighten me," she said, "it won't work. And if I wish to have my cards read, I can do it myself."

Janet stared at her. "Can you? Read the cards?" She was obviously impressed. "Cook can, and Mrs. Finley, too. But neither of them will show me. They say I'm too young." Her voice was filled with indignation. "I know geography and mathematics and all the kings and queens of England in order! I am sure I can recall the meanings of the cards."

"Perhaps," Grace said gently, "what they really mean is that you are not yet ready to know your future."

Janet cocked her head. "Perhaps I am not. But you can do *your* future." She took the deck and handed it to Grace.

Grace took the chair beside her. It had been many years since one of the other junior teachers at Miss Cranmer's Academy had shown her how, but she still remembered.

"I learned on a deck with many pictures, but it's easy enough to do with any set of standard cards. I will take three." She picked up the ace of clubs. "Aces are beginnings and clubs are the same as Wands. They stand for opportunities. So it means the beginning of a new enterprise. In this case, it means my marriage to your father, and the new relationships that will grow from it."

Janet looked at her. "That's one meaning. But Wands also mean strife and discord."

"Well, I see you know more about it than I realized." Grace smiled. "But it is all in how one looks at things, isn't it? If you choose to look for strife, that is your business. I prefer to look on my coming here as the start of a new life for all of us. Now I shall take another card."

She picked one up and turned it over. "There, you see? The nine of hearts. The 'wish card.' All good things come true."

The girl laughed. "You're clever. I like that. Cousin Elspeth is not very clever, you know."

"She seems quite intelligent to me. Why do you say such a thing?"

Janet eyed her with a peculiar expression. "If Cousin Elspeth were as clever as she thinks, then she would be my new stepmama. She always meant to be, you know. Indeed, I think she would have succeeded—if not for you."

"I am sorry if her hopes may have been disappointed, but you shouldn't say such things. You cannot know if you are right."

"Elspeth is in love with my father. She believes that you have stolen her rightful place at Rossmor."

Grace was startled out of discretion. "I'm sorry if that is how she chooses to think of it!"

The girl stared at her. "I don't think one can choose about such things. You love someone, or you don't."

"Yes. Yes, I suppose that is true."

"I have tried to love Cousin Elspeth most sincerely," Janet said, curling a strand of hair around her finger. "But I cannot. Except, you know, in a dutiful way." The blue eyes, so like Alistair's, regarded Grace intently. "Do you love my father very much?"

The change of pace caught Grace off guard. She felt her cheeks grow hot. "Yes. I do."

"Perhaps I should be glad you've come, then. Because I love him very much, too. I want him to be happy. When I was little he was always happy," she said wistfully. "Or so it seemed. But now I wonder . . ."

"Don't look to the past, Janet, but to the present and the future. I will do my best to make you both happy," Grace said. "If I fail, it will not be for lack of trying."

The girl cocked her head. "Yes, you're clever. I didn't think I would like you, but now I am not so sure that I won't." She stacked the cards into a neat rectangle as she spoke. "And I have just realized something wonderful— now that you are here at Rossmor, I am no longer in any danger."

Her words were like a cold splash of water. Grace blinked. "What do you mean? What kind of danger? From whom?"

"From the Gray Lady." Janet slipped the cards into her pocket. "Cousin Elspeth has always been safe, of course. She was never really the mistress here, she only pretended to be. And although she is a cousin, she's not a McLean by either blood or marriage. So the ghost never appeared to her. The Gray Lady only appears to the mistress of Rossmor."

Grace sat very still. "I have heard there is a ghost. Do you mean to say that you really believe in her existence?"

Janet's eyes grew overlarge in her pale face. "I don't 'believe'—I *know*." Her voice dropped to a whisper. "I have been so afraid!"

Grace saw that her stepdaughter was trembling. She leaned forward and covered the girl's hand with her own. "Of what are you afraid, Janet?"

"Why, that the Gray Lady will come for *me*."

"Who has been filling your head with such nonsense?"

"It is not nonsense!" Janet pushed back her chair and

rose. "You don't believe now, but one day you will." She cocked her head again, and her mouth curved up in an odd little smile. She looked far older than her years.

"And now that you have married my father, I needn't worry any longer. *You* have become the mistress of Rossmor—and when the Gray Lady comes, she will come for *you!*"

She fled the room laughing.

By the time Grace reached the top of the stairs Janet had vanished. She decided to explore her new home. The first door beside the solar was locked. The next door led to a small anteroom and the library beyond. It was wonderfully preserved. The ceiling was covered with ornamental plaster in high relief and the paneling was exquisitely carved.

Except for the oriel window in the middle, the opposite wall was row upon row of leather-bound books caged behind slender bars of ornamental brass. Some of the volumes looked very old, but there were newer shelves holding modern books, including several novels Grace had been longing to read.

Two massive high-backed settles flanked the hearth on the left and two matching chairs and a round table of ebonized wood dominated the center of the room. A chess set stood on it, the red and white pieces placed about the board as if a game were in progress. Grace paused to examine it. The red queen held the white king in check.

Two comfortable armchairs of more modern design were pulled up close to the second fireplace, where the claymore of some McLean ancestor was hung upon the chimney breast.

Grace crossed over to it, amazed by its great size. Its pommel was set with polished bloodstone the size of a hen's egg and the time-darkened blade was as long as she was tall. *What was he like, the warrior who wielded such a mighty sword?* she wondered.

She saw him then, standing beside the table, staring down at the chessboard. A red-haired giant with the McLean plaid draped over his shoulder and held in place with a silver badge studded with polished agate. For all the detail, he was insubstantial, like a painting on the air.

As she watched he became as solid and real as the floor beneath her feet. Leaning down, he moved the white queen across the board and smiled in triumph. *Checkmate.*

Grace stumbled back and bumped into a chair. The man was instantly alert, his blue eyes calculating the danger. "Who are ye?" he demanded, rising to his full height. "Why do ye haunt this chamber?"

"I am not the ghost," Grace cried out in fear. "It is you! You!"

He reached out to catch her sleeve, staring at his hands in wonder as they passed through it. She saw the startlement in his face before he dissolved into dust motes dancing on the air. Glancing down at the chessboard again, she saw that it had been no illusion. The white queen had indeed been moved.

Turning on her heel, she fled the room and ran blindly down the corridor. Grace didn't stop until she reached a dead end and was forced to retrace her steps. She'd lost her sense of direction completely. Was the staircase to the right or left? Her breath came in great gasping sobs and her only rational thought was to put as much distance between herself and the apparition in the library as possible.

She took another wrong turn somewhere, and came to a stairway going up. Rather than go back past the library, she hurried up them.

Braedon said there is a connecting door on each floor between this section and the new wing. I will find it. I must find it!

The narrow stairs led up to a series of small rooms used

for storage. Old furniture and trunks filled most. The one on the end had a small window with a dusty casement of thick glass rondels. There was no way to look out without opening it. The catch was difficult but she managed at last.

She leaned out as far as she could, dirtying her hands and the front of her dress in the process. Her hopes of getting her bearings were dashed. There was nothing to see but gables and chimney pots and the moor rising up beyond them.

Her panic increased as she went along the narrow corridor looking for the door to the new wing. *There it is!* Grace hurried toward it and lifted the latch. Instead of the new wing, she found a stone staircase with steps winding down into gloomy shadows on her left hand, and up toward a diffused light on her right. She realized that she had stumbled on the original fortified tower. The glow from above must be light from one of the window slits cut into the thick stone walls.

Grace laughed in relief and stepped onto the landing. It would be easy to find her way back from the foot of the tower. All she had to do was reach the bottom and let herself out to the terraced courtyard.

She went out to the landing. A simple rope strung from circles of iron set into the wall served as the only handrail. It seemed pitifully inadequate, given the steep pitch of the stairs, but there was nothing for it. Lifting her skirts with one hand and grasping the rope with the other, she began to descend.

She felt it before she reached the third step: a terrible grief, a deep, numbing cold that pierced her to the bone. Her teeth chattered as the heat drained from her body and her limbs grew clumsy and stiff.

Grace stopped in her tracks, afraid to move. Glancing up, she saw that the glow at the top of the stairs had grown brighter. It was flowing down the steep steps, like a luminous fog. Fear gave her wings. She flew down the stairs to the lowest level, grasped the door handle and pulled. The door wouldn't open. She yanked again with both hands, but still it didn't budge. *It's locked! Oh, God! Oh, God!*

Despite her terror, she became aware of the darkness receding around her. The eerie light had followed her. Found her.

She raced back to the upper floor, heart pounding fit to burst her ribs. The fear that struck her was beyond reason and she cried out and pounded on the ancient wood until her fists were sore.

The door jerked inward suddenly and she fell forward with it. It hadn't been locked at all: in her panic she'd tried to open it the wrong way.

McLean caught her as she stumbled over the threshhold. "Grace! What the devil? You're white as a ghost!"

She went into his arms and clung to him, warming her chilled body against the heat of his. "I . . . I was lost. I . . . I couldn't open the door!"

He lifted her chin and scrutinized her face. "And that had you beating upon it and screaming like a madwoman? Why didn't you just go down to the ground level and out to the courtyard?"

"I . . . I did! It was locked!" She shuddered and buried her face against his jacket.

He shook his head. "There is no lock on it," he said slowly.

Chapter Seventeen

The sun was high in the sky the following morning, but Grace was still abed. Alistair had spent the night reading with the sitting room door ajar. She had been comforted by the light but would have felt better with him beside her in their big bed. He sat on the edge of the mattress. "I hope you will remain here until I return."

"Really, Alistair, you must not treat me like an invalid! I was lost and got a little rattled yesterday. I am perfectly well."

"Humor me a little longer," he said, leaning down to brush his lips against her temple. "The inquest won't take long. It will be adjourned as foul play by person or persons unknown."

"You haven't told me what Meg said when she heard the news of our marriage."

"I was too shaken when I found you." His smile was rueful. He reached inside his coat pocket and pulled out an envelope. "She sends you this."

Grace took it and broke the seal eagerly. Her smile grew as she scanned the lines of perfect copperplate. "Dear, dear Meg! She is delighted with the news and welcomes me into the family as her sister. Well, I must say I am gratified she took it so well."

McLean laughed. "If she were not so elegant, you might

say that she squealed like a happy piglet when she learned of our marriage. She instantly forgave me the letters that went astray, and promised to call upon you today. I'll stop by and tell her to postpone her call until tomorrow."

"Oh, but I so want to see her!"

Grace argued but lost. "I am adamant," McLean said, taking her hand in his. He saw the stubborn set of her chin. "Give me this small concession, my dear. One day of rest. Think of it: we've been traveling for weeks, we arrive to a household knowing nothing of our marriage, and then you become lost in the tower your first morning here. It's no wonder you became overwrought."

She had to admit it sounded logical. "Tomorrow," he added, "Meg may descend upon you with those two hellcats of hers with my blessing. But today you must rest and recruit your strength."

"Very well. But I will not remain abed any longer."

"Promise me you won't do any more exploring of the house on your own as yet."

Grace shuddered. "You have my word."

He kissed her cheek and went off to the inquest.

Grace dressed and went down to the drawing room, and was disappointed to learn that Janet had gone into the village with Elspeth to purchase some ribbon. She wished they had invited her to go along. She picked up a book of poems from a side table and leafed through a few pages, then set it down. Suddenly she couldn't bear to stay inside the walls of Rossmor another minute.

Alistair can have no objections to a stroll through the gardens.

She rang for her hat and shawl, intending to enjoy what was left of the late-booming flowers inside the sheltered garden; but when the brick walkway divided she chose the way that wound down to the sparkling loch instead.

The water was a deep delphinium blue, reflecting the hills and clouds, and a path wound along beside it. It lured her on. As she crossed the lawn a young collie bounded down to greet her, wolfing and prancing with joy.

"Are you wanting to accompany me?" Grace leaned down and scratched its ears. The dog grinned up at her and wagged its tail. "Very well," she said with mock severity. "But I refuse to toss sticks for you to chase. It is beneath my dignity."

The dog wagged its plumed tail faster. "All right," Grace said, laughing. "But only when we are out of sight of the house."

Grace was soothed by the dog's uncritical companionship. They started down toward the water and the farther they got from Rossmor the higher her spirits grew. She eyed the path. "Come," she said to the dog. "Let's go exploring."

White swans graced the shallows. They ignored the playful yips of the dog and turned back, gliding silently toward the deeper water. Disappointed, the collie had no choice but to follow Grace. From time to time he nosed an interesting scent and took off over the meadows, but he always came frisking back again.

After a brisk walk, she came past a stand of trees and saw a huddle of buildings in the far distance. The village of Rossmor had looked small and unprepossessing from her bedroom window. From this vantage point, however, she could see that it continued on along the shores of the loch. Beyond the shops and houses flanking the main road, the hillside boasted a straggle of small stone houses with flowers in window boxes and gardens in the rear. The moors rose up steeply behind them.

She strained her eyes and made out a large house of elegant proportions below the crest of the moors. That would be Gorse Manor, which belonged to Alistair's uncle.

Suddenly the dog took off like a cannonball. A rabbit bounded up out of the tall grass and the chase was on. "Come back!" Grace called. "Oh, bad dog!"

Rabbit and dog vanished over a rise and she decided to turn back.

A man on horseback was coming up along the loch. For just an instant she thought it was Alistair, but he proved to be a stranger. Although his hair was white, his face deeply tanned and lined with age, his eyes were the same startling color as her husband's. He reined in and doffed his hat as he came abreast of her.

"Good morning. Was that True I saw bounding off through the grass?"

"I am afraid that I don't know. I am new here."

"Yes. You must be my nephew Alistair's new wife," he exclaimed warmly. "I am his uncle, Gordon McLean."

"My husband has spoken fondly of you, sir. You live at Gorse Manor."

"Yes." His eyes twinkled. "I hope that young rascal hasn't been filling your head with stories of my adventures?"

Grace smiled. "No, indeed. Are they very bad?"

"I have never thought so. But then I wouldn't, would I?" He swung down from the saddle to walk beside her.

"I only know that you are a widower, sir, and have spent most of your life sailing the seven seas. In fact, Alistair thought you were visiting your son in Canada."

"So I was." His face creased in a wide smile. "Expensive young rascal! Compared to him I was an angel in my youth. I returned home only yesterday, and found Alistair's letter waiting for me. I rode over to pay my respects, but Braedon informed me that you were out. I am glad now that I took this way home."

"And so am I, sir. It is pleasant to have company on my explorations."

"You've come quite a distance."

"Have I?" Grace stopped and glanced back in surprise. With its crenellated battlements, Rossmor looked like a toy castle in the distance. "Good heavens!"

"Don't worry, I'll show you a shortcut back."

"I don't mind the exercise. Not when the view is so spectacular."

Gordon McLean made a sound of contentment. "Magnificent country, isn't it? Although I imagine in the winter months you will find it isolated and dreary. We do not have the attractions and gay social life that London can offer a young lady such as yourself."

Grace tried not to smile. "I have not been about much in society of late," she told him. "Indeed, I think I will have more than enough to occupy me here."

"Yes. Janet will keep you on your toes," he replied. "She has led Elspeth a merry dance these past three months while Alistair was gone, so I hear. She needs a firm hand. The girl is too much like her mother."

The opportunity to learn something about Finnula McLean was too good to pass up. "What *was* her mother like?" Grace asked.

"Finnula? Moody and morbidly overimaginative. To put it baldly, she made Alistair the very devil of a wife, if you'll pardon me saying it." He smiled kindly at her. "Is that what you wanted to know?"

Grace felt her face burn. "Perhaps it was not a very tactful question to put to you on our first meeting. But you see, Alistair never speaks of her."

"You need not guard your tongue around me. I am a blunt man. I like to see the cards all laid out upon the table, myself. And it is only natural that you should be curious about your predecessor. What else would you like me to tell you?"

She was rather embarrassed and hunted for the right words. "I don't wish you to think that I am prying. It is only that, not knowing anything of her, I am afraid of . . . of perhaps doing the wrong thing and stirring up painful memories."

"I see. You are a woman of exquisite sensibilities. Have

you been wondering how you would fill Finnula's place at Rossmor?"

She nodded.

Those eyes, so very like Alistair's, regarded her thoughtfully. "You can't. Nor should you even try. She was Alistair's first love, and a man never forgets that. But it was a most unsuitable match. Everyone else could see that the marriage was headed for disaster from the start." He rubbed his jaw. "It's no wonder it ended as badly as it did."

She lifted her eyes to his face. "How *did* it end?"

Gordon McLean looked taken aback. "No one has told you?"

"I know very little. Only what Lady Helena has related to me."

"Oh, so you've already met her?" He walked along in silence for a few yards. "Helena is a fascinating creature. At one time I thought perhaps she and Alistair would make a match of it. But their temperaments are too much alike. Both of them stubbornly single-minded and persistent in pursuing their private goals."

She sent him an inquiring look. "You make that sound more vice than virtue, sir."

"Not at all! Certainly I don't mean to criticize your husband. He is my only nephew and I am very fond of him. But I don't believe that partiality should blind one to another's flaws. When Alistair wants something he leaves no stone unturned until he achieves it. Anything that stands in his way will be removed."

Grace stopped and turned to him, her green eyes wary. "Are you trying to warn me of something?"

He looked very uncomfortable. "No. I shouldn't go so far as that. But there is one thing you should know: despite the rumors, and whatever it is that Lady Helena told you, my faith in Alistair has never wavered. I have known him, boy and man, these thirty-some years and I will say it to your head—he had nothing to do with Finnula's unfortunate death."

Grace schooled her features but her heart lurched. "Lady Helena said the same."

"There, you see? It does no good to listen to rumors and speculation." He indicated a path leading up from the water's edge. "This will take us to a point halfway between Gorse Manor and Rossmor. Tell me, what do you think of the old place?"

She wanted to ask more about Finnula—how she died—and why anyone would possibly hold Alistair responsible. But the constraints of good manners prevented it.

"It's extraordinary. I am afraid that—until now—my life has been rather ordinary. I am new to Rossmor and to my role as chatelaine of the manor. I would be grateful, sir, for any advice you may have that will help me in finding my way."

"I expect that Elspeth Lachlan will be your best guide in such matters. I also suspect that she will have some difficulty in handing over the reins to you. I don't imagine she ever expected to do so, in any case. An awkward situation!"

"Indeed it is. You are very astute, sir."

"Well, you may count on me to help smooth things over." They walked along in silence a while. "You married my nephew in Rome, eh? At the embassy, was it?"

"No. Alistair and I were married at a lovely old church in the Borgo."

He looked surprised. "Ah. I didn't realize that you were a member of the Church of Rome."

"I am not, sir. I was baptized and confirmed in the Church of England. But you see, Alistair was due to leave Rome and there was no time to arrange for a Protestant marriage in a country so profoundly Roman Catholic."

Gordon's eyebrows rose even higher, but he didn't comment. They had come to a narrow track intersecting the

path. "I'll leave you here," he told her. "Follow it through
the copse and you'll come out near the stable block. You'll
be able to find your way to the main house from there."

She gave him her hand. "I hope to see you soon at Ross-
mor, Mr. McLean. Perhaps you might come to dinner one
evening this week? Tomorrow, if your plans allow?"

"I should like that. But you must not stand on such for-
mal terms with me. I hope you will call me by my given
name as Alistair does—and give me leave to do the same
now that we are family."

"Of course I do."

Gordon regarded her steadily. "Meanwhile, my dear girl,
do not worry about either Finnula or Elspeth. You are the
mistress of Rossmor now. It is *you* who will set the tone
for the future."

She smiled. "You are very kind and encouraging. I thank
you for it."

"It is my pleasure to be of any assistance that I can."
He kissed her hand. "And tell that young nephew of mine
that I approve of his choice."

He mounted his horse and rode away, with a wave of
his hat. Grace went on along the way he'd shown her, feel-
ing more settled than she had since her arrival. In Alistair's
uncle, she had found a friend and ally.

Turning their conversation over in her mind, she was
halfway to the copse when she heard her name called softly.
"Grace . . ."

She looked around, thinking it was Gordon McLean who
spoke; but she could see him in the distance, cantering
along the track to Gorse Manor. There wasn't another soul
in sight. Somehow, in the next few minutes, she lost her
bearings. The path had given way to stony ground studded
with hardy weeds. She would have to climb the hill ahead
to spy out the lay of the land.

After cresting the hill she stopped to rest in the shade
of the copse. It gave a fine view of Glen Ross and the

wooded valley that widened on the outskirts of the village. She spied a church steeple among the thick trees, and the gabled roofs of a large house. *The vicarage where Meg lives with her family.* And off to one side, a churchyard with lines of tilted headstones like a well-bred matron with a mouthful of crooked teeth.

She recognized it instantly and totally: this was the place of her haunting dreams.

Grace tried to convince herself otherwise. She remembered Alistair and Count Borromini speaking one evening of the experiments of Max Wundt in Leipzig, and of how the mind played tricks, blending memories of past experiences with the present, to produce the phenomenon known as *déjà vu*. Perhaps the details of the dream in her memory were being overlaid by details of the similar scene before her.

But there was the black obelisk, an exclamation point of grief against the blue sky. She stood frozen for a long time, fighting the urge to walk to the churchyard and examine the obelisk at close hand. It was so strong it frightened Grace.

She had to know . . .

She descended the hill to the lych-gate. The cold iron with its the cracking paint and gritty rust, felt real enough beneath her gloved fingers. She pushed it open and entered the churchyard. There were the rows of staggered stones, just as she remembered. The graveled path that led past the dark yews.

Grace approached the obelisk. The black stone pierced the sky, bleak and ominous. She looked for an inscription but the side facing her was blank. Stepping around the monument, she stopped short with a startled cry.

There was the angel, wings outswept and its inhumanly beautiful face turned toward her. Marble tears glistened like tiny pearls upon its smooth white cheek.

Grace felt as if she were caught up in a nightmare. The

air seemed to thicken and her limbs grew heavy as stone. She forced herself to walk around the obelisk and read the inscription chiseled into its square base:

Finnula McLean, Beloved Wife and Mother

Elspeth was crossing the hall when Grace entered. She paused, then came forward. "These are yours now," she said, withdrawing a silver chatelaine from her pocket. She undid the fleur-de-lis pin that kept the chain and dangling keys pinned inside and held it out to Grace. "I hope you will prove worthy of the honor."

Grace recoiled as if she'd been slapped. It took only a moment, however, to collect her thoughts. Her experience teaching had taught her to deal with would-be bullies quickly and decisively.

"My husband is fond of you, Mrs. Lachlan, and so I had hoped we would be friends," she said. "However, it is plain that you have decided to dislike me. I am sorry for it, but I will not let your attitude intimidate me. Nor, may I add, will I permit you to undermine my position. There can only be one mistress here."

The other woman's mouth dropped open. "Well," she said after a moment. "You are very blunt. I will be equally so. Do you wish me to leave Rossmor?"

"No. If you are thinking that I wish to be rid of you, you are wrong. Rossmor has been your home for several years. I hope it may continue to be so. But if we cannot regard one another in friendship, let us at least act with outward respect."

Elspeth flushed. "You are generous. Very well. I will try my utmost to make the transition as easy as possible—for both our sakes."

"I cannot ask for more," Grace said. "And I shall do the same. I met Gordon McLean while out walking and invited him to sup with us tomorrow. I hope you do not object?"

"How can I?" Elspeth replied wryly. "You are mistress here and must do as you think best."

"Where is Janet?"

"Gone up to her room to fetch a book."

Grace excused herself and went up to seek the girl out. She stopped by her own room first and picked up the packages she'd purchased for her. She found her stepdaughter curled up in a window seat, staring out at the loch.

"Are those for me?" Janet asked eagerly.

"Every one of them. I chose them especially for you." She handed her the first package, and was pleased to see that Janet was thrilled with the blue glass beads. "To match your eyes," Grace told her.

The comb and brush were a great success, but the clever little box was clearly the favorite gift of all. She showed Janet how to open and close the secret drawer. "To hide all your treasures and secrets," she told the girl.

Janet colored and set the box down on the window seat. "You went to a good deal of trouble to find gifts to please me—and they do. Very much so." She looked up at Grace anxiously. "I am sincerely sorry that I was so horrid to you earlier."

"We'll start afresh and say no more about it, then." Grace kissed Janet's cheek, and left the girl to enjoy her gifts, encouraged by the way things had gone between them.

Now that she'd begun to make peace with Elspeth and Janet, the future looked brighter. *How foolish I've been these last two days. Anyone might suffer from a nightmare or mistakenly try to make a door swing the wrong way. As to the obelisk, why, there might be one in every churchyard in Scotland, for all I know.*

It was only later, as she was making her way down to the drawing room, that she remembered the blank space where the portrait of Finnula McLean had hung. She saw Braedon hovering at the foot of the stairs.

"The picture that was taken down in the drawing room this morning—where is it now?"

The butler sighed. "It has been restored to its proper place, madam." Grace thanked him and went in search of it, aware that he was watching her. The painting was exactly as she'd envisioned it, down to the ominous shadows and the crescent moon upon Finnula's white brow. And no matter how much she rationalized the other strange events, there was no explaining that.

Chapter Eighteen

Grace sat at her writing table in her upstairs sitting room, penning a note to Lady Helena, while Janet worked on her assigned studies. Since this consisted of curling up in a comfortable armchair with an engrossing book, the girl had no complaints.

"Elspeth had me read the dullest things—mostly books of sermons," she told Grace. "This is ever so much more interesting."

Grace looked up and smiled. "I'm glad of that. I wouldn't want you to take reading in dislike!"

"You're clever," the girl said, smiling back. "And you're giving two lessons in one, because I'm learning Shakespeare's stories at the same time."

Braedon entered. "Mrs. Kinsale has come to call, madam. I have put her in the drawing room."

"I'll go down to her at once." Checking her reflection in the mirror, Grace smoothed her hair in place and hurried down to the drawing room.

A young woman rose from a settee. "Miss Templar! Oh, how good it is to see you again."

Grace recognized Alistair's sister immediately. Meg had changed very little since her school days. She smiled and held out her hands. "Dear Meg! How wonderful you look. Fairly blooming! I am so happy you came to call."

Meg wrinkled her dainty nose. "Alistair will be very cross with me. He tried to persuade me not to come today. I promise I will not tire you out."

"My dear girl, I have just tramped halfway to the village and back out of sheer boredom, and am not the least fatigued. I hope you will stay as long as you may. There is so much news to exchange."

They sat side by side on a settee and talked of school days and of Meg's two sons, whom she'd left behind at the vicarage, in charge of their nurse. "They wanted very much to accompany me, but I thought it would be too much. And to be perfectly truthful, I wanted to have this first visit with you all to myself."

"Perhaps you might bring them tomorrow then, if you are free? We could have a picnic luncheon by the loch with Janet."

Alistair's sister beamed. "How comfortable it is to have you here at Rossmor. And how merry we shall all be this winter, while Alistair and my husband are closeted with their experiments!" Meg gave a little sigh. "He is away in Devon now, at the deathbed of his aunt. Poor thing, she is lingering long past her accounted days."

"He has been gone a while, I take it?"

"Four weeks, and bidding to be longer. Not that I begrudge Aunt Maude every day on earth to which the Good Lord has entitled her." Meg's eyes grew bright with tears. "Only it is the first time we have been separated since our marriage. I miss him terribly!"

"I can understand that," Grace told her.

Meg relaxed. "How nice it is to have another married woman to talk with. And it will be like old times, having a house party at Rossmor. Lady Helena wrote to me that she will be one of the party gathering at Rossmor next month."

"Don't remind me!" Grace said with a look of mock horror. "I am dreading it more with each passing day."

Meg's eyes danced. "I had thought that it would be a stuffy scientific group, but if Helena is coming the company must surely be quite lively. I believe Alistair has some sort of surprise up his sleeve. He is being very mysterious about it all."

"The guest list is quite small; however, this is the first time I will play hostess to so large and distinguished a group. Except for those few I met in Rome, they are all strangers to me. I will have to rely upon you—and Elspeth, of course—to help me keep them entertained."

"I should like nothing better!" Meg rose. "Come to the vicarage one afternoon when Janet takes her lessons with my sons, and we will put our heads together on how to do so. And now I must be going, or Alistair will give me a blistering scold!"

"No fear of that. He's tied up with his account books today."

Meg laughed. "It would be wise to stay out of the way until he's through." She departed with promises to return with her twin sons the following day.

Grace knew that Meg was right: no man wanted to be disturbed while he was going through the estate ledgers. But after a while she grew restive. She wandered over to the estate room in the central portion of the house.

She found him with his elbows on the desk, staring blankly out the window. There were open ledgers and stacks of papers everywhere. "Are you dreaming of escaping by that window?" she teased.

McLean looked up. "Would that I could escape my problems so easily. I've just been informed that there is worm in the beams of the tower, and damage to the south gable of the new wing from a series of unusually strong summer storms. I'm trying to juggle expenses about so I can have the place in fair shape before winter."

"It will be quite costly, then?"

"Very. And dangerous. I don't want you or Janet wandering about when the workmen are there. They will be tearing out railings and replacing treads in the staircases. But you haven't come here to be told of dry rot and beetles in the woodwork."

Taking her hand, he pulled her down on his lap. "At least I hope that is not why you're here." He tilted her face up to his and kissed her until she was breathless.

Does he know how he affects me? she wondered as her arms wound round his neck. *I cannot think clearly when he is too near.* She pulled away.

McLean tangled his fingers in her hair and dragged her to face him for another kiss. It was a calculated move on his part, a subtle statement of possession. He released her, noticing how her cheeks were flushed, her pupils dilated with pleasure.

"Much better than going over columns of figures," he said.

"Yes." She leaned her head on his shoulder and nuzzled his neck. "It's such a lovely day! Do you think you could escape your obligations for a little while? Elspeth is writing letters, and Cook has promised Janet that she might help baking tarts for our afternoon tea. I thought it would be a good opportunity to have some time alone with you."

He trailed a finger down her cheek and along her jaw. "So greedy, my dear? So soon?" He glanced at his watch. "Not three hours since we made love."

He was laughing, but it irritated her. She pulled away. "I don't mean that way. I was hoping we could talk."

McLean's eyes grew wary. "What about? The house party? You had better let Elspeth be your guide. She has handled the details before."

Grace stood up and went to the window. The loch was a deep and transparent topaz in the shadow of the moor. The rest of it shone bright as gold. She leaned against the sill.

"Since we arrived at Rossmor you've spent more time with Elspeth than you have with me."

"That's not true . . . if you'll think back to last night, my dear. And this morning." He went to her, his voice soft and cajoling. "If you don't remember, then it is quite a blow to my pride!"

She hadn't quite placed the source of her discontent until he said that. "I remember quite vividly. However, I should like to spend time with you engaged in other ways. We can't always be making love."

"Good God, woman. We're on our honeymoon still!" He lifted her chin with his fingertip and smiled. "We're supposed to be making love as much as possible."

He saw his joke hadn't had the effect he'd wanted. "Would you like to take a walk through the garden? Or, better yet, let's take the sailboat out on the loch. Cook will prepare a hamper of food. It's a perfect day for it. There won't be many more like it in the Highlands this time of year."

"A sailboat! Yes, if you promise that you won't overturn it and dump me into the loch. I cannot swim an inch."

"I will swear an oath not to let you tumble overboard. And to give you my undivided attention for the rest of the afternoon."

"A tempting offer. I see that I really have no other choice."

Half an hour later they were out on the loch, sailing a ribbon of light across water as reflective as a mirror. Grace had never experienced anything like it in her life. The sail was a white swan's wing, carrying them out in glinting arcs, until the battlements and towers of Rossmor were almost lost to view.

"How long is the loch?" she asked as the bow cleaved the bright waters.

"Eighteen miles from end to end, and five at its greatest width."

She looked down into depths as dark as peat. "How deep?"

"No one knows."

He altered the sail and their speed dropped rapidly.

McLean took her north, toward the dark masses of oak and birch and evergreen that rose from rocky isles. "The five sisters," he told her.

"That sounds as if there is a story behind the name."

"Indeed. There were six to start, each one more beautiful and haughty than the last. A ragged stranger came to their father, claiming to be a great wizard set upon by thieves. No one believed him. He begged for the hand of each girl in turn, but every one of them spurned him as too poor and humble—except the last. So he married her and carried her away, but not before he turned her sisters into islands and their hair into the moss and trees you see."

"What of the sixth sister whom he wed?"

His blue eyes were filled with laughter. "I suppose she lived happily ever after. Isn't that the way of fairy tales?"

"It wasn't very loyal of her," Grace said.

His face grew serious. "Perhaps not to her sisters—but she was loyal to her husband."

"It was cruel of him to make her choose."

"Times were different then. You cannot judge them by our moral standards. I wonder if you will agree with my family motto? 'Loyalty before all.' "

She shook her head. "Not before honor."

"Sometimes they are inextricable."

"The right thing is sometimes done for the wrong reason. But a wrong thing done for the right reason must always be wrong."

He smiled down at her, but there was sadness in the unfathomable depths of his eyes. "The people of Glen Ross fought and died for a lost cause, because they had sworn an oath of loyalty. For that, many of them lost their lands in the clearances, and the right to speak their own language or wear the McLean tartan. A way of life was forever destroyed."

Grace searched his face. "Their loyalty was to a principle, not to a person."

McLean brought the sailboat to one of the islands, where the water lapped against an ancient wooden dock. He made it fast and held out his hand to her. Once they were safely on shore, he took her arm and led her over the rocks until they stood beneath the leafy branches of the trees.

Despite the shelter of their arching limbs, there was a peculiar sense of desolation to the place. Grace was extraordinarily sensitive to it. "This is as good a place as any," he said, setting down their picnic hamper.

Grace took out the bread and sliced ham and cold chicken while he opened the wine. In any other place, she would have been glad to linger on such a lovely afternoon; but there was something about this island that got under her skin, leaving her edgy and anxious to be done.

After she'd repacked the basket, he rose and held out his hand. "Come, there is something I wish to show you."

He led her into the midst of the trees. A massive rock stood alone in the clearing, black as the haunting McLean obelisk in the churchyard, a crude symbol of a bird and a jagged lightning bolt etched upon it.

Her uneasiness grew. "What is this place? I don't think I like it much."

McLean put his hand at her nape and steadied her. "This is the burial site of the man reviled as the Black Laird. He was the husband of Freya, the daughter of the Fair Maid of Ross. The rock was brought down from the mountains at great labor. It was placed there in the belief that it would prevent him from rising up from the grave to seek vengeance."

"Ah. He was murdered?"

"That depends on which way you view the matter. Some say he was justly executed. The McLeans had fought at

Bannockburn with Robert the Bruce, and later at Flodden field for the Stuarts. During the '45, the Black Laird led the men of Rossmor at Culloden, in support of the Jacobite cause. They trusted him. But at the decisive moment he betrayed them and their cause, so that he might keep Rossmor and its vast lands. The men of Glen Ross were led into a trap and slaughtered like helpless sheep."

Grace shivered. "A terrible story!"

"Are you cold?"

He pulled her into the circle of his arms, and she felt the heat of his nearness enfold her like a warm cloak. Her heart quickened. Nothing—not even that fearsome cairn of stone—had the power to frighten her as long as he was there beside her.

She leaned her cheek against his shoulder. "How did the traitorous Black Laird meet his own end?"

"Not in the agony of battle. He returned to Rossmor and died in his bed—at the hand of his own wife, while their young children slept in the room below."

"His wife! How shocking." She pulled back.

McLean's face hardened. His voice rang through the cool, clear air like steel. "Freya was the daughter of a Norse warrior and Frida, the Fair Maid of Ross. Until this century the estate passed down through the female line, and she was captain of this branch of the clan by hereditary right. The protection of the clan and dispensing of stern and swift justice were among her sworn duties. Was it murder, therefore—or an execution? Where should her loyalties have lain, with her slain people or her husband?"

"That is a question only a Solomon or God Himself could answer. I don't pretend to have such wisdom."

His gaze was intense. "Then tell me this: what would you have done in her place? Right or wrong—here would *you* have placed your loyalty?"

Grace pulled her warm shawl more tightly around her shoulders against the chill breeze off the loch. Her voice came soft as a sigh. "With those innocents whose welfare was entrusted to me."

"Yes," he said. "There was no other choice."

Her answer had pleased him and yet Grace felt him distancing himself even further from her. How very different Alistair seemed here. As if a stranger had put on the mask of a familiar face. She tried to shake off the fantasy.

"What happened to Freya afterward?"

"She went to her children and kissed them tenderly and told them she must go away." A muscle ticked in his jaw. "Leaving them in the care of her old nurse, Freya went up to the battlements on the old tower, and threw herself over onto the rocks below. She died instantly."

Grace was stricken. "But what of her children? How could she have left them?"

McLean's face was somber. "Some say she never did."

It took a moment for his words to sink in. Her eyes went wide. "I understand you now. This is a ghost story. And Freya is the Gray Lady of Rossmor."

He looked out across the water. "So it is said. It was then that the legends of the Gray Lady was born. Some say she stays on as guardian of the place to expiate her sins, warning those who come after her of impending disaster. Others say she will walk until the McLeans wipe away the stain of the Black Laird's betrayal. It is our great and enduring shame."

"You cannot take the blame for one man's actions, Alistair! Certainly not one who has been dead almost a hundred and fifty years!"

He shook his head. "I am the McLean of Rossmor. It is my responsibility to see to my clansmen and women. Many of those who survived the massacre were removed from the land during the clearances. Some emigrated to America, others to Africa. Every farthing that I can wring from the estate—yes, and my father before me—has gone to buy up their land that was confiscated, in an attempt to bring the scattered families back."

"I see." Grace put her hand on his sleeve. "It is a noble endeavor, Alistair. I promise I will no longer begrudge the time you spend working to right this wrong."

He felt as if a weight had been lifted from him. His face softened and he lifted a hand to touch her cheek. "I should have known that you would understand."

"I will always try my best to do so," she said.

He looked at her strangely then, she thought. As if he wanted to say more and then thought better of it. A cool breeze gusted in off the water and she drew her shawl closer.

"It's time we headed back," he said. They went back to the boat in silence and he handed her in. She was glad when he cast off the line and raised the sail. *There is a darkness to this place.* And she knew that she would never come back to this particular island willingly.

"Did you bring Finnula here?" she asked.

The question caught them both by surprise. McLean adjusted the canvas and took his time answering. "Finnula came here with me frequently when she was a girl. She and Helena liked to frighten themselves, as children do. Later she developed an aversion to the place. Meg was always less imaginative and more sensible than either of them. She said that once was enough, and after her first visit she refused to go back."

Grace realized that Finnula had sat in this very boat, on the seat where she sat now. It gave her a jolt. She was so in love with Alistair that she had willfully blinded herself to the actuality of his first marriage. Everything at Rossmor must remind him of Finnula. It was a few seconds before she identified the odd feeling that swept over her as jealousy.

Her conscience shamed her. Finnula was dead while she was achingly alive. She had Finnula's husband and the care of Finnula's daughter. *She* was mistress of Rossmor.

She looked out across the loch, sapphire and silver in the bright light, and realized that Finnula had known it in every mood.

Just as she had known Alistair.

She watched him, admiring the strength of his body as he maneuvered the boat with easy grace. The sun brought out the red highlights in his dark hair, the intense blue of his eyes. He was so splendidly masculine, so vital and vibrant, that he made every man she'd ever known seem pale and insubstantial in comparison. Her breath caught in her throat. She wanted them to sail on and on in that clear, golden moment.

Because when they reached Rossmor she would have to come to terms with the truth that was lodged like a festering splinter in her heart: Alistair had chosen Finnula to be his wife, while his marriage to her was the result of an absurd misadventure.

In the depths of her heart she couldn't believe that he would purposely have chosen an obscure governess whom he scarcely knew from Eve, with neither family nor fortune to recommend her, as his wife.

All the pluses were on her side of the ledger. He was everything she had ever looked for in a man. A charming companion. A considerate husband. A passionate lover. Given the choice, she would wed him again in a minute.

But what would he do, if given that same choice?

There. It is out.

As the bow sliced through the water, she held her breath, as if in doing so she could magically suspend time between the tragic past and veiled future.

They reached the dock too soon. McLean made the boat fast and helped Grace out. Her face was pale, her body taut as a bowstring. He thought he understood: she found herself wearing another woman's shoes, and they were pinching her at every step.

She started to move away, but his arms closed tight around her. "Grace. Bide a moment." He took her chin in his fist and raised it until she had to look at him. Her eyes were darkly green and filled with doubts.

"You've been very quiet since we left the island. You are thinking that I see Finnula in every place we go—am I right?"

She shivered. "How can I not? She was a part of your life, and is Janet's mother. I can never take her place."

His mouth tightened. "Finnula is gone. You must make your own place here."

"I will sort it out in time." Her voice shook. "But it is not easy for me."

McLean was touched and exasperated and filled with guilt. There was so much he wanted to say, but couldn't. Not yet.

"I realize it is a trial, and I am sorry for it. I had hoped you would be happy at Rossmor."

"I am. But it is very difficult just now." Grace bit her lip to keep it from quivering. "I confess that I feel like an imposter."

McLean's brow cleared. "That is no doubt the result of our hurried and unorthodox wedding. Exchanging vows in a strange church at the crack of dawn lent the entire proceedings a sense of unreality. That is easy enough to remedy. As soon as Hugh Kinsale returns home, we'll have an official blessing of our marriage—better yet, we will renew our vows before him in the parish church. What do you say to that?"

Grace gathered her courage. "I should like it. But that is not the root of my insecurities: you married Finnula for love, and me out of kindness. I understand that, and must try to deal with it. But it weighs upon my conscience."

"Devil take it! My marriage with Finnula has nothing to do with my relationship with you." His fingers closed over her shoulders. "I was a mere boy when we fell in love, and she was only a girl. Even after we wed and she gave birth to Janet, she remained a girl at heart."

He drew her closer and his voice grew low and urgent. "But I am a man of flesh and blood, Grace—and a man wants a woman. I want *you*."

Her heart sank. Not love, but want. Perhaps she expected too much, too soon.

His mouth hovered near hers. "I want you desperately. Now. Come up to our bedchamber, Grace, and I'll prove it to you again."

Want. Need. Never once "love." Grace hid her dismay.

"You forget," she said breathlessly. "Your uncle is due here at any moment. Yes, you see, there he is riding up the drive."

"Damn and blast! Well, there is no help for it."

McLean relinquished her and Grace hurried up the path to the house, preternaturally aware that Finnula had trod this way a hundred times before her.

McLean watched her go and cursed beneath his breath. Finnula was dead and in her grave—and yet she still had the power to ruin his life.

Chapter Nineteen

Grace and Elspeth sat in the drawing room, waiting for McLean and his uncle to finish their after-dinner port and join them. While the older woman plied her needle on a chair cover she was working in the McLean coat of arms, Grace idly turned the pages of a book. The two women had yet to find common ground, other than Alistair and Rossmor, on which to base any friendship.

The door opened and Alistair and Gordon joined them. The four soon fell to discussing the coming house party. "It will be good to see Lady Helena again," Gordon commented. "She used to be a frequent visitor to Rossmor before—" He broke off as if he'd been about to say something indiscreet.

"Alistair has invited a medium to enliven things," Elspeth announced into the awkward silence that fell. "A Mrs. Dearing."

Gordon turned to his nephew. "I have heard of her through friends. But I am surprised that you would want her at Rossmor."

"She is an acquaintance of Count Borromini. I suspect she is a charlatan," McLean said. "If so, I shall expose her during the séance."

"Up to your old tricks, nephew?"

"I don't know what you mean."

Gordon wasn't intimidated. "It is evident that Mrs. Dearing believes she is to participate in a joint experiment—while the true experiment will be your attempt to expose her."

The discussion was interrupted by Braedon's sudden appearance. He coughed discreetly. "You are wanted in Miss Janet's room, Mrs. Lachlan."

Elspeth set down her embroidery and rose. Grace was concerned. "She went up to bed hours ago. She is not ill, I hope?"

"She occasionally has difficulty sleeping," McLean said. "Elspeth is always able to settle her down."

He was proved wrong when Braedon returned in less than ten minutes. "Your pardon, Mr. McLean. Mrs. Lachlan has asked for you to join her."

"I'll come at once." He put his hand on Grace's shoulder. "It is nothing, my dear. From time to time my daughter suffers from nightmares. I will go up to her now, if you will both excuse me?"

"Of course you must go to her," Gordon replied. He bowed to Grace. "Meanwhile, I shall spend the time making better acquaintance with your delightful bride."

After the door closed behind McLean, Gordon went to a side table. "I almost forgot: I borrowed this book on West Indian customs from Alistair and intended to return it before I went to Canada."

Grace recognized the title. "There is a second volume to this subject. I saw it in the library only today."

"Is there, by Jove? Excellent. I'm afraid this one did not contain all the information I required."

"Come along to the library, then, and I'll find it for you." She led the way to the older section of the house and True followed faithfully at her heels.

"The dog has taken quite a shine to you, Grace."

"He's my shadow. Except when Janet is about. Then he

is false to his name: he abandons me the moment she rubs his head and practically grovels at her feet."

She kept up a stream of conversation all the way to the library. It was the first time she had been this way after sundown. The servants had lit the lamps in their glass sconces along the way. It seemed a great waste of oil to have so many lamps burning; but the farther they went from the new wing, the more her opinion changed. There was something eerie about the place, and the lonely echoes of their footsteps. She would not willingly come here alone after darkness fell.

While she rummaged among the titles on the shelves, Gordon strolled over to a glass case. "Ah, the Peiping Bowl. It is my favorite of all my grandfather's collection."

Her heart stopped and skipped a beat when he opened the case and took out the fragile item. The bowl was twelve inches across, carved from precious jade of gray and white. The sides were intricately pierced around the rim, the rest so delicate and fine that light shone through as if it were stained glass. She was afraid he might drop it.

"Perhaps you should put it back before True leaps on you," she suggested gently. "I don't trust him to behave himself."

"Nonsense. He's a good dog." Gordon turned the bowl toward the light. "As for myself, I'm in the habit of dealing with fine jade and porcelain wares. At one time I was involved in the import trade. I've quite a collection up at Gorse Manor. You remind me to show it to you when you visit."

"I should love to see it," she said, and heaved a sigh when he replaced the bowl as lightly as if it were formed of the cloud it resembled.

He examined a butterfat jade snuff bottle with a carnelian cap. "This is new." His fingers caressed the smooth sides with the appreciation of a connoisseur. "I must say that Alistair has as exquisite taste in Chinese artifacts as he does in wives."

"Heavens! You make him sound like Bluebeard."

"Good God! My unfortunate tongue." He set the snuff bottle back inside and closed the door. "What I meant, my dear, is that you do him proud. Rossmor has never looked better."

"I cannot claim credit for that. It is due to Mrs. Finley's ministrations and to Elspeth's care. Indeed, I am struggling to fill her shoes."

"How do the two of you march along these days? Is her nose still out of joint?"

"I can answer for myself, Gordon." Elspeth stood in the doorway, her face as flaming as her hair. "My nose, as you can see, is perfectly in line. However, my temper is drawn rather fine at the moment."

"So I see." He bowed to her. "You know my blunt ways, Elspeth. I spent too many years at sea to bother with the formalities. I say what is on my mind and in my heart."

"Do you, Gordon?"

He lifted his head and looked at her. Grace watched the strange byplay between them and felt the tension in the air.

The moment passed. Elspeth brushed past Gordon and pushed against the door of the glass case. It clicked shut. "You hadn't closed it properly," she admonished him. "Alistair must see that the broken lock is replaced."

"Grace said you took excellent care of Rossmor. I wish I had someone to look after Gorse Manor even half so well."

Elspeth flushed. "I would suggest that you place an advertisement in the Inverness newspapers!"

She swept out, and Gordon took his leave shortly afterward. Grace wondered if there had been some sort of romantic attachment between Alistair's uncle and cousin at one time. It wasn't an unreasonable assumption. There was no blood relationship, for Elspeth was related to Alistair through his mother, and Gordon was a fine figure of a man, still in his prime.

Perhaps they will make a match of it, she thought. She liked the idea. If Elspeth were happily married and mistress of Gorse Manor, she would forget her grudge against Grace. Perhaps, in time, they might become friends.

After seeing Gordon off, she went upstairs. Alistair wasn't in their bedchamber, so Grace went along the corridor to Janet's room.

The girl sat upright in the bed beneath her coverlet of white and blue. Her eyes were wide, her skin pale as wax, but she seemed calm. Every lamp and candle in the room was lit, and a hearty fire leapt in the hearth. Not a single shadow lurked in the corners of the room.

"May I come in?"

"Janet was just asking for you," McLean said. "I have given her a mild sedative."

"Is that wise? She is just a child."

A faint frown formed between his brows. "A short time ago she was a very hysterical child in acute distress! And I, need I remind you, have a degree in medicine."

"Of course. How foolish of me." Grace sat on the other side of the bed and took the girl's hand in hers. "I understand you had a bad dream?"

"Oh, yes. I was so frightened, I cannot tell you! I was in the tower, climbing the stairs, and I heard someone coming up behind me." Her voice quavered as she relived it in her mind. "Then I awakened—and she was here in the room with me!"

McLean's face was hard but his hands were gentle as he brushed a loose tendril of hair from her face. "It was only a dream, darling."

Janet leaned forward. "No. It was not a dream, Papa. I swear it."

Grace picked up the book on the nightstand beside the lamp. "Shall I read to you until you grow sleepy?"

"I should like that," Janet said with a faint smile.

"Very well. 'Once upon a time there was a Selfish Giant . . . ' "

McLean waited until Janet's eyes closed and her breathing deepened. Grace smiled and nodded for him to leave, thinking the girl was almost asleep. She read on for several minutes, then let her voice drift away. She placed her hand on Janet's forehead and brushed back her hair.

The girl's eyes opened sleepily. "Oh! I thought it was *her!*"

"Were you having another dream?"

"It wasn't a dream," Janet whispered. "She was really here. I could smell her perfume."

Grace's heart gave a sickening lurch. "That is surely unusual. I have never heard of a ghost that wore perfume."

Janet turned on her side with her back to the light. Grace had to lean down to hear her reply: "Mother always wore perfume," she murmured. "Lavender and roses and something else . . ." A few minutes later she was sound asleep.

One of the maids had been assigned to sleep on the truckle bed in case Janet awakened in the night, and Grace left to seek her own bed. She hurried down the corridor and didn't pause till she was safe in her own bedchamber.

McLean came out from his study in a dressing gown. "How is she?"

"Sleeping soundly."

She wanted to ask him about Janet's strange words, and why she feared her mother's ghost; but he pulled her into his arms. Her face was already angled for his kiss. Her breasts ached with yearning.

"This is the time of day I like best," he murmured into her ear. "When we are alone together and the world does not intrude."

"I, too. I've missed you these past few days, Alistair, when you have been so preoccupied with the estate."

"Is that what it is?" He lifted up her chin and kissed her.

"You feel ignored? Well, my dear, I intend to devote a good deal more attention—beginning here and now . . ."

His lips were warm against the angle of her jaw, his hands caressing as they ran lightly over her curves. One cupped her breast as his thumbnail traced intricate patterns over its tip. Grace sighed with pleasure. The intimacy of the gesture, the low pitch of his voice stirred her with sensations. With images of his naked body gleaming in candlelight as they lay entwined amid the embroidered sheets. With fevered memories of his touch upon her flesh and her own, wanton response to it.

He undid the blue ribbons that tied her gown together and slipped it from her shoulders to pool at her feet. His hands reached out to take the ribbon from her plaited hair, and tugged it all loose. It fell down her back like a silk curtain.

"Beautiful Grace," he said softly. "Do you know what you do to me with a touch, a glance, the gentle swaying of your body against me? You drive me mad! I want to devour you."

His mouth skimmed over her shoulder and down her breast. He suckled gently, then pulled and tugged and nipped with his strong teeth until she moaned with need. He was alert to every sensation that shuddered through her. She was burning with desire.

A fever of need shook Grace. Heat rose from her belly, licking over her skin like tongues of flame. Her questions and worries went up in smoke. Ghosts, secrets and rumors all receded from her mind. There was nothing but the hard, lean length of him against her, and the fire that leapt between them.

Her body felt liquid and as insubstantial as the moonbeams that fell across the floor. McClean swept her up and carried her to the bed. She curled against his chest, weightless in his arms. He felt every tremor that went through her body. Knew that she wanted him with primitive urgency that matched his own, and he exulted in it.

He placed her on the bed and blew out the candle. Moonlight illuminated her, silvered her rounded shoulders, the sweet globes of her breasts, the graceful line of hip and thigh.

She watched him strip off his dressing gown, and her mouth went dry with desire.

How magnificent he is! She imagined the crisp dark hairs of his chest brushing across her breasts, the strength of his arms about her, the way his hands stroked and teased and incited. She moved against the soft sheets, arched her back, raising her arms above her head.

His breath caught in his throat. Her witchy hair was spread out on the pillow like a veil. He fisted handfuls of it, slid his fingers through it, reveled in its sensual texture, its deep, arousing scent. "I think you have cast a spell upon me."

McLean stretched out beside her and cupped her breast in his palm. He could feel the quivering of her body, the wild beating of her heart. There would be no languorous foreplay this time. There was no need of it. She was as impatient for the consummation as he.

Grace wanted him with such fierce hunger that nothing else mattered. If they were still downstairs in the drawing room, she would have felt no different. Instead of the moonlit bed, she would have let him take her on the carpet in the glow from the hearth.

Want built to need, need to such wild desire she had no control over it. Over herself. She reached up eagerly as he straddled her and lowered himself over her. Welcomed him with all the passion that welled up from the deepest reaches of her soul.

Their joining was fierce and free, a dark rapture that caught them up and whirled them, slick and gasping, into its fiery heart.

Later, when they were cast up on the still shore of contentment, she lay with her back to him, within the warm circle of his arms, drowsy and replete.

It was only later, as she drifted to sleep with her body curved into his, that she remembered there was something she had wanted to ask him. Something about . . . It slipped away as softly as the moonlight on the floor.

Grace awakened in the night, groggy and shrouded in the echoes of fading dreams. She sighed and rolled over on her back, then realized the other side of the bed was empty.

The light of the moon poured through the uncovered window. The shadows of the mullions lay across them in dark contrast like the bars of a jail cell. Grace got up to close the curtains and gasped. An apparition hovered on the far side of the room: a disembodied face with a mouth like a gaping wound. She froze in place, too terrified to move.

The door from the corridor opened and candlelight filled the room with wavering shadows. "Alistair!" she exclaimed.

He went to her side, setting the lit taper down on the bedstand. "I went to peek in at Janet. She's still sound asleep."

"Look! Over there in the corner."

He laughed. "You are as foolish as my daughter. It is only your own face reflected in the looking glass."

She laughed, too, but with embarrassment. "That is twice since we've arrived here that I've made a fool of myself."

"It's only natural. I've learned that expectations color observations. Even the most objective scientist can be tricked by them. You've heard rumors that Rossmor is haunted, and Janet imagined earlier that she'd seen a ghost. Your sleeping mind combined the incidents into the dream from which you've only just awakened, and it projected the expectations of that dream onto your waking interpretation of reality."

"It sounds perfectly logical when you explain it," she said, trying to quiet the rapid pummeling of her heart against her ribs.

He got into bed beside her and pulled the blanket up. "I'll hold you until you fall asleep."

Grace snuggled against him, letting the warmth of his body seep into hers. With his strong arms around her, she felt protected, even from the power of dreams. As she drifted into slumber, she was vaguely aware of a familiar fragrance: rose and lavender and bergamot. Of a light, gusty exhalation.

It sounded very like a woman's sigh.

Grace awakened from a dream near dawn. It seemed urgent that she recall it, but the details faded away like mist. Rolling on her side, she discovered that her husband was awake, as well. He stood by the bed looking down at her. "What is it? Has Janet had another nightmare?"

"No. She hasn't stirred, the maid said when last I checked. I thought I heard you cry out in your sleep." He removed his dressing robe and slipped beneath the covers. "I wondered if you were having a bad dream."

"I don't remember any of it—but I don't know if I can fall back asleep again."

"Well," he said, pulling her against his chest, "I have the cure for that. Since we are both awake and in bed . . ."

He kissed her and she reciprocated with all the passion he could want. When he touched her all doubts vanished and there was nothing but the two of them, alone in the indigo shadows of the bed.

His hands slid down and covered her breasts. His palms

brushed lightly, and he felt the quick, quivering response. He'd never expected such ardor from her. Each time he was amazed. He rolled over, pinning her beneath his weight. "Beautiful, beautiful Grace."

He nipped at her shoulder, moved lower, and she curved up in delight for more. As his hands caressed and roused, she wound her arms around him. Her breathing quickened and her body arched up, eager for his touch. He teased her with his tongue, taunted her with deliberate prolonging of every movement.

She was dizzy with desire. He told her that she was beautiful, that she drove him to the edge of madness and beyond. Grace prayed for something more. *Tell me that you love me, Alistair. Tell me that what we have between us is more than physical need.*

His lips skimmed from the hollow at her throat to the curve of her breast, while his hands smoothed over the sweep of her hips to the tender, silken skin of her thighs. But he never spoke the words she longed to hear.

The heat of his mouth, the stroke of his fingers, drove everything else from her mind. There was nothing but the glow of the banked fire, the slow, intensely sensual rhythm of their lovemaking. The growing urgency and pounding need. The sudden, spangling flight that shattered her with its brightness.

They slept and wakened, kissed and slept again. Just past dawn they made love a second time, this time hot and hard. She wrapped her legs around him, raked her nails down his back, dared him to take her faster and higher than before. Sweat-slicked and wild, they reached the crest together, their deep cries muffled by their breathless wonder.

A chambermaid, hurrying silently past their room, smiled and shook her head. They were a lusty pair, the master and mistress. She'd never heard the like!

Chapter Twenty

Grace sat before her mirrored dressing table while Cait combed through her damp hair. Her thoughts were not on the reflection in the looking glass, but on her predecessor. No one seemed to have the same image of Finnula McLean.

Lady Helena Ainsley had called her lively and charming, Gordon McLean had hinted that she was moody and morbidly over-imaginative, and Meg had spoken of her as gracious and beautiful and beloved by all. The Finnula that Elspeth had known was quiet and fragile, and she kept any other opinions of Alistair's late wife to herself. Mrs. Finley, the housekeeper, clearly had adored her, and, as for Braedon, trying to pry a morsel of information out of the old butler had been as fruitful as milking a rock.

Grace sighed. Which Finnula was the real one?

The facts she'd gathered were few. She had been the only daughter of an aristocratic union and had grown up in a grand house, although nothing on so large a scale as Rossmor.

While Grace had been teaching at Miss Cranmer's, Finnula had been the toast of London. "Books of sonnets were dedicated to her, and artists vied for the opportunity of painting her," Meg had said with a wistful sort of pride.

Grace smiled wryly. *I am not exactly an antidote, but I can't imagine anyone writing sonnets to me.*

Elspeth shrugged. "It will be worth it in the end. His aunt is quite wealthy—and though Hugh is sincerely attached to her, I cannot help but think that his devotion has been enhanced by the possibility of being named her heir. He has no other income, and is dependent entirely upon the living of St. Declan's. Which is to say, Alistair's generosity."

"I imagine it will come in quite handy with two boys to educate and set up in the world," Grace replied.

Elspeth checked the monogrammed gold watch pinned to her bosom. "Well, I must leave you to your toilette. There are matters which I must discuss with Alistair. Have you and Mrs. Finley gone over the arrangements in the tower for Count Borromini yet?"

"I am meeting her in a half-hour's time to do so. Although why anyone would want to sleep in a haunted chamber where a murder was committed, is beyond me."

Elspeth gave a short laugh. "When you get to know Alistair and his friends better, nothing will surprise you. They will go to outlandish ends to further their experiements in occult phenomena. We are none of us safe from them!"

She left with a graceful swing of her skirts. Elspeth was a very attractive woman. Grace frowned at her reflection. It seemed that three or four times a week Elspeth and Alistair closeted themselves away in his study, to "discuss something." It made her feel very much an outsider in her own home. *What business could they possibly have together that requires them to spend so much time alone?*

She was amazed by the wave of sudden jealousy, and a little ashamed. But Alistair brought out such strong feelings in her that at times they were a little frightening.

Janet came in and sat down on one of the chairs, swinging her legs. "I'm bored. I wish it was time to go to the vicarage."

"If wishes were jewels, we all would be decked out like queens."

"Yes." Janet swung her heels. "My mother and I used to play a wishing game. If you could have your dearest wish, Stepmama, what would it be?"

"I don't know. I cannot think of anything I lack."

"There must be something."

A husband who loves me . . .

But she shook her head. "I am the most fortunate of women. The only things I've ever truly desired were a home and family of my own, and the leisure to indulge my vice for reading. And I have those now, you see."

Janet's eyes met hers, and then her lids came down to hide their expression. "Mama used to wish for all sorts of things."

"And what were they?"

"Once it was for a singing nightingale made out of gold and jewels, like in Mr. Andersen's story. Another time it was to have wings to fly like a bird. I remember that she used to go up to the tower when it was warm like today, and let the wind blow through her hair to dry it. She said it made her feel as if she were flying."

The girl picked up a porcelain trinket box from the table and examined it. "Mostly it was to live in London in a fine house and go to balls every night, like she did when she made her come-out. She said she would go mad if she had to spend another winter snowed in at Rossmor."

She set the box down. "Will you go mad?"

Grace shook her head. "I am sure I'll find enough to keep me occupied. And that reminds me: After we return from the vicarage, I thought you might like to help me with the sachets for the guests' rooms. I finished sewing the last of the satin sacques for them yesterday evening."

Janet looked surprised but pleased. "I would like to— only I don't know how."

Grace smiled. "Then you will learn. I've noticed that you are very quick when we play at jackstraws. Perhaps you might pick out the lavender stems from the blossoms."

She saw the beginnings of a sulky look on the girl's face. "Then as a reward I'll give you even more work—if you like, I'll let you sort the rose petals."

"Really? Elspeth never lets me help." Janet's eyes sparkled and all sullenness was banished. "May I help stuff the sachet sacques?"

"And tie them with ribbons too, if you like."

Janet thought a moment. "I suppose I have nothing better to do."

Grace tried not to laugh. The girl was so transparent, so eager to be liked—and so quick to rebuff any overtures. "If anything more entertaining should present itself, I won't hold you to it," she said.

She expected Janet to leave then, but the girl sat on the edge of the bed, absently stroking True's head. She seemed lost in thought.

"Is there anything wrong?" Grace asked. "You've seemed preoccupied of late."

Janet met her gaze solemnly. "I had another nightmare. But it was different this time. I dreamed about the churchyard. We were going there to put flowers on my mother's grave."

"Would you like to do that? We could stop on our way to the vicarage."

"I don't know." She lifted her head and Grace saw the strain in her face. "There is a marble angel near it. In my dream, when I passed by the angel frightened me. There were tears like milk sliding down its cheeks." Her voice dropped. "And it spoke to me!"

Grace was stunned. The resemblance to her own recurring nightmare was uncanny. The comb fell from her suddenly nerveless fingers, knocking over a small cut-glass scent bottle. She retrieved it clumsily from among her lotions and perfumes. "What did it say?"

"I don't know. I can't remember . . . but my mother had the same dream, I think. I heard her tell Papa that she went to the churchyard and the angel spoke to her. I am not supposed to know of it." Janet glanced up anxiously. "You won't tell, will you?"

"No, my dear. It will be our secret."

"Thank you!" The girl jumped off the bed. "I am so glad I told you about the dreams. I . . . I don't know why, but I feel better now."

"I'm very glad that you do."

Relieved of the burden of her nightmare, Janet kissed Grace lightly on the cheek. "I will be in the garden with True when you are ready to leave."

Grace watched her in the mirror until the door closed behind her. *Here is a mystery!* She and Janet and Finnula had all dreamed the same dream. *It is impossible. Unless . . . somehow, Alistair is the link between us! But what does it all mean?*

She rubbed her temples. The whole thing was too disturbing. She didn't want to think about it.

In the past weeks she'd learned her way around the old house. The door at the end of the corridor was a shortcut, opening to the upper gallery of the old hall. She slipped through it. The panelling and the ceiling beams had been waxed and buffed to a soft glow. She passed the gallery where the crimson curtains had been beaten of their dust, and opened the door on the far end.

She was in the tower, on the second landing. Her heart beat a little faster at her daring. She hadn't ventured here alone since her first day at Rossmor. Grace waited with the door open, to see if any remnants of the past lingered. There was no stir of memories, not a single echo or strange glow. The tower felt empty and safe, and she started up.

Scant light fell through the window slits, but she could see how the center of the steps were worn from the generations of feet that had trod upon them. The first slit gave a view across the meadows to the sudden rise of moorland. There was the vicarage, and just beyond it the churchyard where Finnula was buried. She could even make out the gables of Gorse Manor through the trees. Gordon McLean's home was large and comfortable, and filled with wonderful treasures from his travels.

Another circle of the tower brought her to a window with a view of the loch. It was as still and smooth as polished silver. Another turn, another door. Grace paused. This was where the infamous Black Laird had met his end. She'd never been this high up before alone. She decided not to venture inside until she had Mrs. Finley's company.

The door opened suddenly and she gave a stifled shriek of surprise. Mrs. Finley peered out. "Ah, there you are, madame. All is in readiness."

Grace smiled. "Rossmor could have no finer house-keeper than you, Mrs. Finley."

"And a joy it is to have the caring of it. I fell headlong in love with the old place the first time I set eyes on it when Finley—God rest his soul—brought me here as a young bride. He was head gardener, you know. 'You'll never get me out of here again except feet first,' I told him."

"Let us hope that day is far off," Grace said. The house-keeper chuckled.

"I've no plans of going anytime soon, be sure of that!"

Grace became aware of a scent: rose and lavender and bergamot. A chill rippled through her. "What is that lovely fragrance?"

"That would be the potpourri. Miss Finnula made it every summer from an old receipt she found in the still-room."

Grace examined the chamber's only furnishings: a carved-wood bed with a high brocade canopy, a small night-table, two low chests and a table and two chairs of ebonized wood. *Certainly Spartan, compared to the splendors of the Palazzo Borromini,* Grace thought. But the count had insisted that nothing be changed from the original. Once Grace gave her stamp of approval, the house-keeper whisked off to her appointment with Braedon.

Instead of following her, Grace was emboldened to go up. She opened the low door that led to the battlements and stepped out, leaving it ajar. A brown bird gave a startled cry, flapped its wings and flew away. The sun was warm, the wind soft and sensual as a lover's touch.

She went to the parapet and stood in awe. The view commanded the entire glen, from the rolling moors and distant mountains, to the toy village sprawled along the loch. A sudden gust of wind snatched her lace cap away. Her hair tumbled loose, dark locks streaming back behind her like wings. If she stretched her arms out, she would take flight, soar out over the silver-blue water with the sun warm on her back. She lifted her arms to the wind, tipped her head back and closed her eyes. A wild surge of elation poured through her. It *was* almost as if she were flying.

And then suddenly she *was*. A hard blow struck her between the shoulder blades, pitching her forward and into the gap between the walls of the rampart.

She fell against the stone and the force of it knocked the breath from her lungs. She lay there on the edge of nothing, terrified and fighting for breath. Below her was seventy feet of dizzying nothing—and there at the bottom, sharp-toothed rocks rising up through the dark water at the tower's base.

There were footsteps behind her. Her heart pounded so loudly she couldn't tell if they were running toward her or away. The next instant rough hands seized her shoulders. She was yanked up and lifted completely off her feet.

Grace screamed and kicked out. Her lashing foot connected with something solid. There was a grunt of pain, but an arm like steel wrapped around her waist. She seemed to hang in the air for eternity, waiting to be hurled helplessly over the parapet and dashed down upon the rocks.

She was jolted to her feet, pinned against a hard, muscular frame. Surrounded by a familiar scent. "Alistair!"

He spun her around to face him. He was livid with fury. "What the devil were you trying to do?"

"I might ask the same of you! You almost sent me over the edge."

"I pulled you back, you little fool! Mrs. Finley told me you'd come up here. I found you hanging halfway over the parapet."

Grace was trembling violently. She scanned his face. His anger and fear seemed as real as her own. "Oh, Alistair! I was so frightened. Someone hit me hard between the shoulders, and I lost my footing."

He glanced around. "You must have tripped. There is no one here but the two of us."

Her shivering grew stronger. "I know what I felt! Someone shoved me. Hard!" She burst into tears of fear and anger. "Who would do such a thing?"

"Calm down," he said, smoothing his hand across her back. "You're safe." And he pulled her into his embrace.

She felt the thud of his heartbeat as if it were her own, the sheltering strength of his arms. He smoothed her hair and she thought for a moment that he meant to kiss her. Instead he smiled stiffly and released her.

There was a great flap of wings overhead, and McLean looked up. "There is your answer. It must have been one of the birds that nest up here," he said. "It swooped in so swiftly to land, that it flew right into you."

Grace shook her head and held on to him tightly. "It didn't feel like a bird. It felt like a hand!"

"I've seen birds shatter windows from the force of their speed. Come," he said. "We'll go down and I'll fix you a cordial to restore your spirits. Perhaps it would be best if you say nothing of this to anyone."

She was stunned. "You don't believe me, do you, Alistair?"

"My dear, you must see that it would cause a good deal of comment. You say you were pushed—and I tell you that there was no one else up on the battlements."

Grace fought her rising anger. "Are you saying that people will think I am making up bizarre stories merely to be interesting?"

"They are just as likely to say that it was I who pushed you," he told her. He eyed her coolly. "Is that what you believe?"

"No! Of course not." Nor did she want to start any more unfair rumors about her husband.

McLean's jaw tightened. "Servants gossip—and Janet is young and very impressionable. I don't wish her to be frightened again, now that she is just beginning to sleep well."

Grace softened immediately. "I understand. I will say nothing of it to anyone."

He tipped her face up to his. "It isn't safe up here, my dear. You must promise me that you will never come up here alone again."

Grace shivered in the chill October breeze. "You have it willingly!"

He released her, smiling. "Look! There are two feathers where you were standing. I imagine the bird suffered as great a shock as you when the two of you collided."

She turned and saw the glossy gray and white feathers, and a little fluff of down at their bases. Relief left her light-headed. What had she been thinking, to doubt Alistair even for a moment?

As he held the door open for her, she took a last glance over her shoulder, and caught a glimpse of something moving against the stone, just beyond the edge of her vision. Gray on gray, like layers of mist.

She blinked and it was gone.

Grace put the incident in the back of her mind as she and Janet rode up to the vicarage. "You're right," she told her stepdaughter. "The pony will soon be too small for you, and you are a good enough rider to have a horse on which to hack about. I'll speak to your father."

She couldn't have said anything that would have brought a brighter smile to the girl's face. Then the door to the ivy-covered stone house opened and two red-haired boys came running out onto the wide side porch. "Janet! Janet! You must come see the clever toy Father sent us from London! It does all manner of clever things."

They stopped shyly when they saw Grace, and sketched her quick bows. She was a prime favorite with the twins. "But first," she said, "let me guess which of you is which." She spied the tell-tale scab on one's lip. "You are Angus, of course—and you are Geordie."

Meg's boys were awed. "No one can tell us apart except Mother and Father!"

"Well, now you know that you cannot fool me either," Grace told them. "So you must not waste your efforts in trying."

"We wouldn't do that," Angus declared. "You are a great gun!"

"May we take Janet up to the nursery and show her our new toy?" Geordie asked. "It is a hand-powered engine, and can spin tops or make sparks on a friction wheel or . . . or, well, a great lot of other things besides."

"Of course. And I have brought a fresh batch of scones from Cook to have with your tea."

Meg ushered Grace inside. "You must tell me what you think of the new curtains and slipcovers. I do so hope that Hugh will like them."

The cozy parlor had been done up in William Morris fabric of subtle gold and black scrolls on a royal blue background. The two armchairs beside the fireplace were re-covered in blue velvet and the windows hung with gold. "My dear Meg, it is enchanting! And I like the piano where you've moved it over by the bookcases."

She noticed that some photographs had been arranged along the top of the piano and went to admire them. There was a lovely daguerreotype of Meg and a smiling young man who must be her husband, Hugh. A silver frame held one of Lady Helena in full court dress—and its twin one of Alistair with his first wife. They looked young and happy, and she wondered if it had been taken for their wedding.

"I hope you do not mind," Meg said anxiously when she saw that Grace had noticed it. "I had thought of putting it away . . ."

"You needn't do so on my behalf. I am sure it is a comfort to Janet to see it there."

While the children played abovestairs, the two women discussed plans for the coming house party at Rossmor. Meg was eager for any change from her domestic routine, and immersed herself in details. Grace, however, found her attention wandering. She was increasingly distracted by the view from the bow window, dominated by the square tower of the church and the graveyard beyond. Once Finnula had sat here, making plans with Meg. Now she lay beneath the black granite obelisk.

I cannot escape from her, she thought anxiously, and remembered her dreams of the gravestone and the weeping angel. Grace threw caution to the winds. "When I passed the churchyard I couldn't help but notice a tall black monument set off by itself."

Meg smiled and shook her head. "That is one of the McLean markers. Vulgar, isn't it? Grandfather was enamored of all things Egyptian."

"It seems somehow familiar to me. Amazingly so, in fact."

"As well it should. There is an engraving of it that has been much reproduced. There was even a popular song that featured the monument on the sheet music. One of those overly sentimental ones, verging on the morbid: 'My true love sleeps upon the moor,' " Meg sang, " 'beneath a heather quilt.' Quite dreadful!"

Grace was astonished. "I have heard the words and melody somewhere, but cannot place it."

Meg crossed over to the pianoforte. "I believe that there may be a copy of it in the music cabinet. The engraving was used as the cover. Yes, here it is," she said after riffling through a few sheets.

Suddenly she stopped and frowned down at it. Grace rose and went to her side. The engraving of the black obelisk stood out starkly upon the pale lavender paper.

"Of course!" Relief welled up giddily. "I must have seen a copy of this piece of music at least a dozen times. One of the young ladies at Miss Cranmer's Academy sang it for the spring musicale."

Meg hesitated. "I had quite forgotten: it is dedicated to Finnula."

Grace could have laughed out loud with relief. For weeks she'd been haunted by dreams, which she'd taken to be some sort of unexplained and frightening phenomenon, like her vision in the Forum. And all the time the explanation was so simple!

She remembered Alistair and Count Borromini speaking of the experiments of Max Wundt in Leipzig, and of how the mind played tricks, blending memories of past experiences with the present, to produce the phenomenon known as déjà vu.

At some level not accessible to conscious thought, she had connected the dedication with Finnula and the engraving of the obelisk upon its cover. Since she didn't recall any of it in her waking state, her mind had woven it throughout her dreams.

"Meg, perhaps it is very wrong of me to ask—and I will ask you this only once, I swear it. Please forgive me if it distresses you—but I should like to know how Finnula died. Alistair never discusses it."

"Oh! I thought Alistair would have told you." Meg looked away. "She fell from Freya's Tower during a storm."

"Ah. That explains why Alistair was so upset that I went there alone today. He said it was not in good repair."

"Y . . . yes." Meg drew the syllable out. "That is one reason, I am sure."

"But there are others?"

The other woman blushed. "You will think me foolish, no doubt, but I have always avoided it."

"Have you a fear of heights?"

Meg shook her head. "No. It is the Gray Lady. That is where she is said to begin her ghostly walk."

A little shiver slithered up Grace's spine. All the way back to Rossmor later, while Janet chattered of Angus and Geordie and their clever toys, she was aware of Freya's Tower looming above the roofs and gables. Remembering a brief glimpse in the storm that first night of what had looked like a spectral figure on the battlements. In her mind's eye the shape of it became more distinct, the form more solid even though she knew it had been nothing but layers of mist.

Alistair is right. Expectations do color observations and alter memories. I must train myself not to expect phantoms in every turn of the corridor, and ghosts popping out of the woodwork.

McLean poured out two fingers of whisky into a crystal glass and took it over to the window. Janet and Grace were out in the garden with a basket, selecting the last of the late flowers for the drawing room. They had a quantity of late purple asters and chrysanthemums in gold and cream. He watched as Grace added branches from a shrub covered with shiny berries mottled in dark red and wine and palest yellow.

Somehow she would manage to work them all together into a harmonious arrangement, just as she was doing with the household. Janet's initial jealousy was being replaced with growing affection, and Elspeth's dislike had mellowed into a grudging respect.

Not that my cousin will admit it to me, he acknowledged. *Or even to herself.*

He hoped he'd done the right thing. He'd been so sure of himself in Rome, so certain that he knew what he was doing and could handle the consequences. Could handle his own attraction to Grace and the inevitable complications. McLean cursed himself for being a complete and utter fool.

She came up the brick walk halfway toward the window where he stood, but with the sun reflecting from the panes she couldn't see him. It seemed a metaphor for their relationship: Grace, going blithely through the sunshine, while he stood in the shadows.

He downed the whisky neat. The warm, peaty taste of it filled his throat and the fire of it burned straight to his heart. Beyond the glass his wife leaned over and snipped some leafy green stems, her movements as delicate as her name.

This was how he'd always imagined his life would be: work and family and Rossmor. It was all illusion—but just for a moment he could pretend that it was real. That it could last.

The sounds of their voices carried, although he couldn't tell what they were saying. Janet laughed a little too shrilly, and he gripped his empty glass so hard his knuckles blanched. She'd been alternately overexcited or quiet and withdrawn the first few days of his return home. Her emotions had swung like a pendulum, and he wondered what would happen if they swung too far. Finulla had been so at the same age.

There were times when Janet reminded him so much of her mother that it wrung his heart. He remembered all too well how Finnula could be. In tears one minute, bubbling over with gaiety another. Every emotion magnified. Sometimes she had seemed to balance on a razor's edge, ready to fall either way.

A poor choice of words, he told himself, and poured out a little more of the water of life.

When the devil is Hugh Kinsale coming back? Without his brother-in-law, this little charade might not hold together much longer. He wondered what Grace would do if his schemes unraveled.

I should never have set foot on this twisting path, he thought, rubbing his hand over his jaw. *But now that I have . . . I must do whatever is in my power to see it through!*

For Janet's sake.

That night, as Cait was helping her undress for bed, Grace heard the girl gasp. "What is it?"

"Och, madam! You've a great walloping bruise on your back!"

"Yes. A bird struck me when I was up on the battlements this morning."

"A bird dinna cause that mark, madam! I'd swear it on the Good Book!"

Her vehemence made Grace uneasy. "Hand me the mirror, Cait, if you please."

She took the handmirror the maid gave her, and turned around to look over her shoulder at it in the large looking glass on her dressing table. A dark bruise covered a swath of skin in the center of her back and there were several smaller ones just below her shoulder blades.

A chill ran up her spine. Whatever had caused the purple discoloration, she had to admit it looked very like the imprint of a human hand.

Chapter Twenty-one

Grace sat at the inlaid desk in her bright sitting room, going over the household inventory of linens Elspeth had provided her. The house guests would begin to descend upon them at months' end, and there was still so much to do.

She glanced down at the paper covered in neat writing and read it again in bewilderment. Six tablecloths of fine damask, three of lace, four of embroidered linen. So many embroidered sheets, so many plain. Pillowcases of various lengths and descriptions. A goodly number of quilts and spreads and down coverlets.

"Four sheepskin blankets faced with cotton," she read aloud, "one bound in blue cord, one mended in right-hand corner. Sixteen lace and cotton sachets: rose; ten embroidered cotton sachets: lavender. Good God. What in heaven's name am I supposed to do with this?"

True lifted his head and thumped his tail against the carpet. She patted him. "You are fortunate to be a dog, True. All you have to worry about is whether you'll have a nice meaty bone for your dinner."

She consoled herself that even if she seemed to be making scant headway in mastering her duties as chatelaine of Rossmor, at least she was forging ahead in educating her stepdaughter. She was pleased with Janet's intelligence and eagerness to learn, and accompanied her to the vicarage for the lessons that were given there to Meg's twin sons by Mr. Murrah, a retired schoolmaster.

While the children recited their Latin verbs or scribbled away at figures on their slates, Meg and Grace came to know each other well. Their affection was deep and their friendship abiding. Elspeth, however, remained aloof.

Alistair breakfasted with them almost every morning, but after that he was so busy with estate matters and the repairs to the old part of the house that they didn't meet again until they sat down to dine in the evening. It irked Grace that he managed to spend so much time closeted with his cousin Elspeth, yet had so little time for her. It was only after they went upstairs for the night that she had his full attention. Then he was as passionate a lover as any woman could ever wish.

Her own relationship with Elspeth remained civilized but distant.

She hoped this coming house party would help to break the ice between them. On an impulse, she went along the corridor to Elspeth's sitting room. The door was ajar, and she was standing with one hand holding aside the yellow window draperies while she looked out through the panes. She turned slightly but kept her face averted when she heard Grace at the door.

"May I come in?"

The other woman shrugged.

"You are mistress of Rossmor, and may come and go anywhere you please."

"I am. However, this is your room. I won't trespass upon your privacy." She started to retreat, but Elspeth stopped her.

"What is it you wanted of me?"

"I wondered if you would care to go over the final preparations for the house party," Grace said. "You know Rossmor and most of the guests, and you have the expertise of hosting a large party, which I lack. I would be very grateful for your suggestions."

"You will learn as you go. As I did, and Finnula before me."

Grace ignored her rudeness. "I suppose I shall. But in the meantime, it might make things considerably uncomfortable for our guests. I am not asking for myself. I am asking because I wish to do credit to Alistair . . . and to Rossmor."

She saw that she'd selected the right lure. Elspeth wavered only a moment. "Very well. Tomorrow, if that suits you. Not for you or for Alistair, but for Rossmor."

She turned away, dismissing Grace, but that was a miscalculation. Grace had no intention of leaving now until she cleared the air. "I think it is time for the two of us to have a tête-à-tête. You are angry at Alistair for marrying me," she said, "and at me for usurping what you feel should be your role here."

Elspeth's fingers curled tightly about the drapery fabric. "No. Not for that. Perhaps for overturning our quiet little world. I thought we should go on as before when Alistair returned from Rome. Only everything is so changed . . ."

Grace shook her head. "Change is the very nature of life. Nothing can remain unaltered by time."

The other woman was silent and Grace realized that she held a crumpled handkerchief in her other hand. It appeared to be damp with tears.

Grace realized belatedly that what she'd interpreted as coldness in Elspeth's voice had been her efforts to control her emotions, to keep them from spilling over. "What is wrong, Elspeth?" she asked in alarm.

"It is nothing to do with you! I have been thinking of the past a good deal lately," she said. Elspeth gestured to one of the armchairs pulled up before the fireplace, where a low fire crackled against the chill. "Perhaps it would be best to clear the air. Sit down. Please."

Elspeth closed the door and leaned against it. Her eyes were red-rimmed from weeping. "I was married at sixteen and went out to India with my husband. Twenty years ago today. It was the greatest change imaginable, but I managed to survive. I learned to adapt and became a part of an exotic world that was totally alien to me."

"It must have been difficult," Grace murmured.

"It was fascinating and frightening. The houses were strange and servants spoke another tongue, and dressed in white tunics or gossamer silks dyed in a thousand colors. It was a country of paradoxes. There were cobras in the garden—and gorgeous flowers that might have come straight from paradise. One night we heard a tiger roar and in the morning we saw his pug marks in the road. Later that same day we attended a ceremony in honor of the queen's birthday."

Elspeth was totally caught up in her memories, and her voice grew soft and dreamy. "The afternoons were so hot when we arrived that everyone napped through the middle of the day, and the wax flowers melted on my best hat. In the monsoon season we were shut up in our houses while the wild rains lashed the trees and battered the roofs. But I was a young girl and madly in love with a dashing officer. I learned to shut myself away from the strangeness of my new life, and carry on as if I were still in England. I lived in a world that was largely make-believe."

Elspeth knotted her slender fingers tightly around her crumpled handkerchief. "Then Donald became ill. A recurrent tropical disease from which he never quite seemed to recover. He retired from the military on his pension. Gradually our friends returned to England or were posted elsewhere. And then one day, he was gone. So you see, everything changed again. It was a very lonely and distressing time."

"You must have been very young when you were widowed."

Elspeth looked up sharply. "I do not mean he died. I meant that he was gone, literally! Donald left me for a native woman. They lived together quite openly, although they were shunned by the English community. The humiliation of it staggered me. I could no longer remain in India. When Alistair learned of it, he invited me to stay at Rossmor, and I accepted gratefully. Janet was barely out of leading strings and Finnula had just suffered a miscarriage. There were several in the next few years."

Grace was startled. Here was a piece of information that no one had told her.

"When I first accepted Alistair's offer I thought I could make myself useful," Elspeth continued, "and I was looking forward in many ways to returning to my homeland. I was homesick for Scotland. But when I arrived, I discovered that it was no longer home. Instead of cool mountains and rolling moors, I pined for heat and bright colors. For spicy curry and rosewater ices, and the clamor of the bazaars. I struggled so hard to fit in . . ."

She collapsed in a chair, weeping. Grace rose and knelt beside Elspeth's chair. "I am so sorry for dredging up such painful memories. I didn't know . . . Alistair had told me only that you were widowed."

"And so I was," Elspeth said bitterly. "Donald died suddenly, leaving his doxy and son behind. I made no claim upon his estate—but I was so angry! She had a home and a child, while I had nothing that was my own. Nothing!"

Grace held her hand. "I begin to understand you. After Finnula died, you carved out your place here. And then I came along and snatched it away from you. Is that what you felt?"

Elspeth nodded. "But today I realized it wasn't your arrival, it was something more profound. I was not mourning the loss of my position here, but the loss of control over my own life. I had blinded myself to it, substituting Rossmor for husband and family. It was merely a symbol for all my life lacked, but I mistook it for substance. Today Alistair helped me understand that I didn't want Rossmor to belong to me, but for *me* to belong to Rossmor."

"I do understand," Grace said softly. "And you will always have a place here."

"No. I don't want a place *given* to me. I want to *make* a place that is mine. Oh, dear! I am explaining it so poorly." Elspeth dabbed her eyes. "You must think me an utter fool."

"No. I think you are a woman of great sensibility, who is strongly in need of a friend—and a cup of tea," Grace replied in a rallying tone. "Shall I ring for it? Or perhaps something stronger?"

Elspeth laughed weakly. "Something stronger would be in order. For both of us. There is a mead-and-honey cordial on the little table beside the sofa."

Grace found the cut-crystal decanter and poured rich amber liquid into two small stemmed glasses. Light flared from the facets and Elspeth's fingers closed convulsively around the stem. "I warn you, this is not for the faint of heart," she said. "Better to drink it down quickly, and get all the agony of it over at once. Then you can enjoy the aftereffects at leisure."

Grace perched on the edge of the armchair again and sipped from the other glass cautiously. It went down like flaming honey.

The older woman's color and spirits had revived with the cordial. "Perhaps you have wondered what Alistair and I talk about when we are alone," she said to Grace.

"Yes, I admit that I have."

"You know that his research concerns the workings of the human mind, and phenomena for which we have no rational explanation."

"Yes, he had told me that."

"Currently he is putting some of his theories into practice—he plans to eventually publish his research. For the last few weeks, Alistair has been helping me search for the true cause of my distress through the use of hypnotism. During the sessions he encourages me to become relaxed and look at my problems as if from a far distance. Hypnosis, it is called. It has helped me a good deal."

She blew her nose. "Today was what Alistair called my breakthrough. He helped me to see that I am jealous neither of your relationship with him, nor your position as mistress of Rossmor. It is myself I am looking for. My true purpose in life. I wept then as I did now—as if a floodgate had been opened. I feel . . . cleansed and renewed. As if all the debris of my loss and anger has been swept away."

Grace had her own admission to make. "I'm afraid that I misunderstood the situation entirely. I have been so overwhelmed with learning my new role as mistress of Rossmor that I failed to look beyond it."

But in losing Elspeth as a suspected rival, Grace had also lost her explanation as to why Alistair had distanced himself from her. It was difficult to reconcile the aloof, watchful and unfailingly polite stranger with the passionate lover of her honeymoon. Thank God she had Janet and Rossmor to keep her busy. And that was what Elspeth needed, too.

"Until you decide what you wish to do, I hope I may persuade you that I need your help desperately. I promised Mrs. Finley that I would write up a final designation of who is to stay where, but became hopelessly entangled in the protocol. I am hoping that you will take pity on me and help me through it."

Elspeth blew her nose. "If you like, I will come down when I have composed myself, and go over the proposed arrangements with you."

Grace smiled. "I should like that very much, indeed."

"You said once that you had hoped we could become friends . . ."

"Yes. And I still do, Elspeth." She held out her hand, and the other woman took it.

"As do I. You are good for Alistair, and making progress with Janet. She has warmed up to you," Elspeth said, "in a way she had never done with me."

"I can never take her mother's place, but I hope to fill a void in Janet's life. Perhaps, one day, in her heart as well. I am exceedingly fond of her."

Grace paused, then plunged into a topic she had never dared broach before. "No one ever speaks of Finnula but Janet—although Meg told me how she died. What a tragedy."

Elspeth eyed her with dismay. "You must not judge her harshly."

Grace's eyes widened. "I do not judge her at all."

The other woman turned her gold bangle bracelet around and around on her wrist without realizing what she was doing. The tiny rubies in the eyes of the gold lion head on it caught the light like little flames.

"Finnula . . . Finnula was under strain," she continued in a low voice. "She had been upset and out of sorts for some time. It was attributed to her miscarriages. There were several after my arrival, as I've said. She had dreams. Nightmares that preyed upon her mind.

I suppose I must be honest with you. She thought she was being haunted by the Gray Lady. In time she began to believe that the ghost was trying to lure her to her death. I tried to reassure her and Gordon sent over special cordials to help her failing appetite. Not even Mrs. Finley's cakes, which Finnula used to love, could tempt her to eat. We were frantic. Alistair sent for the best experts to heal her— although they were ostensibly at Rossmor as ordinary guests. They held sessions with Finnula, similar to those Alistair conducts with me."

"And did they help her overcome her troubles?"

"It seemed so. She suddenly snapped out of the doldrums. Finnula was almost herself again. Lighthearted and gay, almost to the point of hysteria. Fey, as we say in Scotland. Finnula climbed Freya's tower and leapt to her death. Out of respect for Alistair and the McLean name, the coroner ruled it death by misadventure."

Grace's heart thumped against her ribs. "You are saying that she committed suicide?"

"No one knows for sure what was in her mind except God." She bit her lip. "Alistair awakened in the morning to find her gone. The house and grounds were searched. It wasn't until later in the day that her body was spotted, cast up on the rocks below the old tower."

They were both silent a moment. Grace put out her hand to cover Elspeth's. "I am sorry to have put you through that. But I thank you most sincerely for telling me. Hopefully, the knowledge will prevent me from doing or saying anything to rake up the tragedy."

"Yes. It is best not to speak of it. Alistair blames himself for being too wrapped up in his research to see what was happening to her until too late. He'd thought she was well on her way to recovery. And I blame myself for being too wrapped up in my own misery to be the friend Finnula needed."

"You cannot know that it would have made any difference," Grace murmured gently.

"Perhaps you are right. Leave me now to compose myself," Elspeth said. "I shall come down within the hour and together we'll finish the plans for the house party."

"Thank you. I shall look forward to it."

Elspeth smiled. "So shall I."

True to her promise, Elspeth soon helped sort out the arrangements for the house party. By the time Grace had finished going over the sleeping arrangements for the houseguests and their servants—and the order of precedence at the dining table—her head was whirling.

"It must be so natural to you that you no longer have to think about it," Elspeth encouraged. Grace closed her eyes and recited aloud:

"Count Borromini at the top of the tower, his secretary on the floor below, and their valets in the two small rooms at the bottom. Lady Helena Ainsely in the Rose Bedchamber, Miss Rosenthal in the Blue, and Mrs. Dearing in the Gold Room in the new wing. Professor Rosenthal and Lord Peltersham in the suites above the Great Hall in the medieval wing, and their servants to be housed in the various rooms on the upper floor."

"Very good," Elspeth told her. "And now we must go over the dinner seating."

Grace groaned. "I am thankful this is a small party or I should lose my mind before the guests arrive."

Janet came bouncing into the drawing room. She was wearing a blue riding habit that matched her eyes.

"I'm ready," she announced. She saw the blank look on Grace's face. "You promised we would ride over to the vicarage today."

Grace laughed. "So I did. But you are early."

Janet's face went from sunshine to cloudy in the blink of an eye. Grace pretended not to notice. "I will go up and change into my riding habit as soon as we are finished here. While I am changing, perhaps you might wish to select one of the ginger cat's kittens for Angus and Geordie."

"I should love to! But will Aunt Meg mind?"

"It was her idea. She wanted to surprise them."

"I know just the one! It's yellow, with gray stripes. Or"—she cocked her head—"perhaps the funny little black one with the white paws. But the calico has the sweetest face. Oh, dear. I cannot make up my mind."

She skipped out the door to the corridor just as her father came in from the terrace. "I couldn't help overhearing," he said to Grace. "You have a remarkable way of handling her."

"I am not 'handling' her, Alistair. Janet isn't a pony to be trained."

"If you'd seen her galloping across the lawn not ten minutes past, all stockings and flying petticoats, you might think differently!" McLean's smile turned to a frown. "I was a little short with her, I'm afraid."

"I wish you would not be so hard on Janet! It is only the natural high spirits of youth. There's time enough for her to grow up."

He turned to his cousin, as if expecting her to side with him in the matter; but Elspeth had slipped discreetly away. "The two of you seem to have set aside your differences," he commented.

"We had a long talk earlier. About Elspeth's past—and about your hypnosis sessions. I have been wondering why you never discuss your scientific work with me."

McLean shifted uncomfortably. "I considered them to fall under the same protection as confidences between a physician and patient. There will be enough of that during the house party. As to my general research, I would prefer you to make your own observations and form your own judgments, independent of mine."

Grace laughed. "I have never had a problem with drawing my own conclusions or expressing my opinions. You need not fear I will begin now. In fact, I will tell you that I have been hurt that you have kept so much of your work a secret to me."

"I could not very well discuss Elspeth's problems, spoken to me in confidence as they were, with you. I hope you understand."

"I do now. But if there are other aspects of it you could share, I should enjoy learning about your research and experiments."

He took her hand. "My secretiveness has made you feel left out. I see that now, and apologize for it. You are very important to me, Grace." He lowered his voice. "More so than you can even guess."

"Oh, I do hope so, Alistair! I have been so afraid that you had tired of me, and regretted our hasty marriage."

McLean saw the sheen of tears in her eyes, the faint quiver of her soft lips. He forgot his resolve and pulled her into his arms.

His mouth covered hers, gently possessive, then with an increasing urgency that reverberated through her entire body. She wished for a moment that they were away from Rossmor, just the two of them. He seemed to read her mind.

"I must go to London in early December to address a congress on aspects of my research. Would you like to go with me? We could journey down a week ahead of time, and stay over afterward."

"I can think of nothing I'd like better," she said reluctantly. "But I don't think it would be wise to go away so soon again. For Janet's sake."

Her words shocked him out of their mood of sudden intimacy. McLean released her.

"Then we'll take her along. Yes, and Elspeth, too. I'll hire a house, and we'll return here in time for Christmas," he said briskly. "I'll send a letter to my London agent to find us a suitable place."

The moment was lost. Filled with regret, Grace left to go up and change into her riding habit. *Alistair must think I didn't want to be alone with him.* They were back in limbo. As she was crossing the hall, Braedon appeared at her side. "The post, madam."

Grace reached out and took three letters from the silver tray. The topmost one was from Lady Helena Ainsley, the second from Mrs. Bingley, and the third from Miss Rosenthal.

She took them up to her room and rang for Cait. Grace sat at her dressing table and opened the letters while Cait fetched the garnet riding habit, which she had just finished pressing. Mrs. Bingley's letter was crossed and recrossed, full of the news of her daughter's engagement to Mr. Oliphant, and glowing plans for a wedding in London during the Little Season.

> *Although the recent death of his great-aunt makes a large society wedding impossible, I am over the moon at seeing Liza so happily settled. To think my dear daughter will be marrying a young man so rich in prospects! (He is heir to his uncle, Admiral Leighton, if I have not told you so before.) Although I confess I cannot like their plans to reside in Africa, where the discomforts are myriad and there is no society life as we know it, my dear Mrs. McLean.*

A smile curved Grace's lips as she read on. It was good to know that Mr. Oliphant was no fool. Removing Liza from her mother's sphere of influence would do both Liza and the marriage a deal of good. The postscript jolted her.

> *There has been much talk among the English traveling abroad on your marriage to Mr. McLean. I assured those who spoke of it that he is most civil and gentlemanly, and that I place no conviction in the rumors regarding his first wife's untimely death.*

Grace crumpled the letter in her hand. There it was again, that monstrous scandal aimed at Alistair. And how vexing that Mrs. Bingley, who was usually the font of the most minute bits of gossip, had failed to be more specific. She wondered what circumstances there had been surrounding Finnula's death—whether by accident or suicide—to cast such a long shadow over her husband's reputation.

Grace watched Cait put away the bandbox that had held her smart riding hat with the dashing feather. "How long have you been at Rossmor, Cait?"

"Twelve years now, madam."

"Then you were here when the first Mrs. McLean fell to her death."

"Oh, yes, madam. I had just been promoted from scullery girl to nursery maid to Miss Janet."

Turning toward the mirror, Grace set the fetching hat atop her hair and adjusted the angle. But her eyes were on Cait's reflected image, not her own. She never listened to servants' gossip, but this was different.

"Tell me," she said casually. "Is it your belief that the first Mrs. McLean fell—or that she jumped?"

Cait's face went white. "There be some as say she was pushed, madam."

Grace twisted around on the bench. "Pushed! By whom?"

" 'Twas the Gray Lady. Cook says that she grew tired of guarding the house, and so chose another mistress of Rossmor to take her place."

"What utter nonsense!" Grace said. "It's no wonder that my stepdaughter has nightmares if these are the sorts of things she hears from the servants' hall!"

The maid eyed her stubbornly. "Miss Janet did not hear it from any of us, madam. 'Twas her mother herself who told her of it—aye, and any other body that would listen to her, poor raving, mad creature! And her so beautiful. 'Twas a terrible pity."

Cait recollected herself. "But I should not be nattering on about what is over and done with, and long past mending. Will there be aught else, madam?"

"No, thank you. You may go, Cait."

The girl whisked out of the room before her mistress could ask her any further awkward questions. Grace sat there thinking over what she'd said. The more she heard of Finnula's demise the more confused she became. Now she had three versions of the event and a couple of dramatic twists. Depending on who was relating the story, Finnula either fell, jumped in a fit of despondency, or was purposely pushed either by the malignant family ghost—

Or Alistair.

And if Finnula had truly been insane then suicide seemed the most likely option. Grace wondered if her condition had inspired Alistair to abandon physical medicine for research into the triumph and frailties of the human mind.

The mantel clock chimed softly, and she collected her thoughts enough to read through the other two letters she'd received. Lady Helena's note was short. It took Grace a moment to read it, as the writing was exactly like Lady Helena herself: a bit dashing, very elegant—and more complicated than was first apparent.

She wrote that she looked forward to seeing Grace again, sent her fond regards to Alistair, Elspeth, and Janet—and hoped it would not inconvenience them unduly if she arrived "a few days in advance of the other guests" as had been her frequent habit in the past, since she was already in Scotland and "it would be a great folly to travel all the way back to London only to turn right around again."

Grace stared at the date of her proposed arrival in shock. Lady Helena intended to come the following day, a full week before the other guests.

Good heavens, how will we manage to entertain her until the others arrive? There aren't enough people in the neighborhood to provide her with the kind of social stimulation to which a woman of her station is accustomed!

She broke the wafer on Miss Rosenthal's letter last, thinking as she did so that perhaps she might invite them to come in advance of the other guests as well. According to Alistair's accounts, Professor Rosenthal and his daughter were charming, well informed, and witty: exactly the kind of company Lady Helena would appreciate.

But as she scanned the flowing lines of writing, Grace's spirits sank. Miss Rosenthal sent her most sincere regrets; her father had been taken ill in Vienna quite suddenly, and while a complete recovery was almost assured, he would not be well enough to attempt the rigors of travel for several months.

Grace went into the sitting room and immediately dashed off a reply, sending good wishes for the professor's full recovery and hopes that they would be able to visit Rossmor at a future date.

As she was gathering up her things, she became aware of an overwhelming fragrance of rose, lavender, and bergamot. She looked around uneasily. A scratchy whisper made the fine hairs at her nape stand on end and sent spiky shivers up her spine:

Grace.

The heat was draining from the room as if an arctic wind blew through it. Her blood chilled. *Grace!*

"Who is it who calls me?" she cried out defiantly.

Finnula . . .

The sound of the dead woman's name in that breathy exhalation filled Grace with cold terror. "Why?" she demanded. "What is it that you want?"

A sigh echoed through the room. *To warn you . . . that you will be next . . .*

Grace didn't stay to hear more. She fled the room and almost collided with her husband.

He grasped her arms. "What's wrong?"

She held out Miss Rosenthal's letter still gripped tight in her hand. "I . . . I was coming to tell you. We have a change in plans. Lady Helena is arriving tomorrow, and Professor Rosenthal is too ill to travel, although expected to recover eventually."

"The devil you say! Poor Ernest!" McLean released her. "And I was coming to notify you of another defection: Lord Pettersham has been appointed to head a diplomatic post of extreme delicacy which he cannot in good conscience refuse. He regrets that he will be leaving for South America, and does not expect to return before the New Year."

Laughter bubbled up inside Grace. "That leaves only Lady Helena, the count, and Mrs. Dearing. Here I was dreading cutting my teeth as a society hostess—and now we will be woefully short of guests and my greatest feeling is disappointment. There is no pleasing me!"

She looked so disappointed that McLean drew her into his arms without thinking. "Isn't there?" His mouth was warm on hers, his hands exciting as they skimmed over her face, her throat, the soft rise of her breasts beneath her jacket. "You're wearing one of those new French corsets," he whispered against her ear. "The topless one. I like it very much."

"Do not like it too well," she laughed, fighting the temptation to surrender her plans. "Janet is waiting for me. We are expected at the vicarage at any moment."

His voice was low and teasing. "Then you must wait for tonight to see how well I intend to please you."

Another kiss and he released her. "Until this evening . . ."

Her cheeks were flushed when she came down the stairs, just thinking of it. But on the way to the garden where Janet was waiting, she glanced up at Freya's Tower. Something moved behind one of the arrow slits. Who would be up there at this time of day, now that the restorations were completed?

A shiver came over her as she remembered that eerie voice, and its icy warning. Grace cursed her unexplained abilities, wishing that she could see only what was tangible, touch and smell and taste only what existed in the here and now.

She hastened along the brick walkway, unaware that two undergardeners saw her pass. One of the men scratched his head. "Will ye look at the mistress there? Pale as tallow. Do ye ken as there might be a wee laird on his way?"

"Aye," the older of the two said thoughtfully. "It's possible. Or else the poor lass has seen a ghost."

Chapter Twenty-two

Grace and Janet rode toward the vicarage on a picture-perfect afternoon. Cream-colored sheep grazed on the golden moors above them and down below the loch was a gleaming smear of Prussian blue. On any other day it would have filled Grace with a sense of tranquility, but she was too disturbed to appreciate it.

Grace had a fair idea of how prevalent the rumors had been following Finnula's death. She wondered why they had started in the first place. Was it because Finnula was so young and lovely, and her death so tragic? Or had there been other reasons? Gordon McLean had hinted that his nephew's relationship with his first wife had not been perfect, yet among those closest to him Alistair's devotion to her was never doubted.

Grace realized that Janet was speaking to her. "I'm sorry. I was off woolgathering."

Those blue eyes, so like Alistair's, regarded her gravely. "Something is worrying you. Is it the house party? I can help, you know. Perhaps I could come up with anagrams, or titles for charades."

"An excellent idea," Grace said, "although I fear we will run out of guests long before we run out of ways to entertain them." She explained it all to Janet and saw the girl's keen disappointment. "At least Lady Helena will be with us, and she is coming tomorrow."

That news perked Janet up immensely. "I do like Lady Helena! She is like Uncle Gordon and never makes me feel as if I should be hidden away somewhere in the nursery."

"Elspeth's notions are a little old-fashioned, but she is coming round."

As they turned into the drive of the old vine-covered vicarage, they realized that a carriage was pulled up to the front door.

"It must be Uncle Hugh!" Janet slipped down from her pony and handed the reins to the stablelad. She managed to untie the basket from her saddle and was at the door before Grace had even dismounted.

Meg met them on the porch, her face flushed with joy. "Come in! My husband has only just returned."

"Perhaps this is not a good time for us to call," Grace protested.

"Oh, no. Hugh is most anxious to meet you."

She ushered them into the neat parlor where Angus and Geordie were wound around the legs of a tall man with fair hair and laughing brown eyes. He disentangled his sons, gave Janet a quick hug, and came forward to Grace with his hand extended.

"My dear Mrs. McLean, I am most happy to make your acquaintance at last."

"And I, to meet you, sir." He'd sent Grace a warm congratulatory note upon hearing of her marriage to Alistair and his presence radiated the same good nature.

"Now that you've had time to settle in, what do you think of Rossmor? Is it sufficiently old and haunted to please your notions of romance?"

"It is a unique and fascinating manor."

He must have heard something in her voice she hadn't intended. The dark eyes scrutinized her. "You sound unsure."

"Merely a catch in my throat," she said quickly.

"I'll see to the refreshments," Meg said. She smiled at Janet. "Now, what can it be that you've brought in that basket? More scones, perhaps, for our tea?"

Janet smiled shyly and set the basket down before her cousins. "Something even better." She lifted the lid and a gray tabby kitten peered over the rim, then tried to climb up and tumbled out onto the carpet. The two boys were ecstatic.

"A kitten! Can we keep her?" Geordie asked, picking up the ball of squirming fur. "What's her name?"

"Can we give her a saucer of milk?" Angus wanted to know.

"It is not a 'her,' but a *him*," Grace told them, "and you must decide between you what to call him. He is very fond of milk."

"Why don't the three of you come into the kitchen with me, and we'll find a dish of milk for the dear little creature."

The children went off eagerly, carrying the mewling kitten with them. After the commotion of their arrival, Grace found herself alone with Alistair's brother-in-law. He came to her side and spoke with odd intensity.

"Meg has written me a good deal about you, Mrs. McLean, telling of your many kindnesses. I feel I know you quite well."

"Then I hope you will not stand on ceremony, but call me by my given name."

"And you must call me Hugh." He gave her a conspiritorial smile. "After all, we are the outsiders here and must stick together. I noticed your hesitation earlier when I asked you about Rossmor. Has anything occurred on the premises to upset, or possibly to frighten, you?"

"Forgive me," Grace said, "but that is a peculiar thing to ask."

"Is it?" His gaze was shrewd. "A young bride should be

happy and content, not nervous and abstracted. And, given your special psychic abilities, it would be no surprise to learn that you have experienced some unnerving contacts with what is euphemistically called the 'other side.' Perhaps even a visitation from the Gray Lady herself."

She felt the color drain from her face. " 'Special psychic abilities . . .' "

"Should I not have mentioned your particular gifts? Forgive me if I have offended you. However, since such matters are the basis of Alistair's research, I thought you would have no objection. We discuss such matters quite openly among ourselves."

"I am at a disadvantage," she said, brazening it out, "since I am not sure how much Alistair has told you."

She was making it up as she went along, trying to pull information from Hugh without letting him know that she was very much in the dark. It worked.

"Alistair and I have long shared an interest in such phenomena," Hugh said. "I received a letter from him during his visit to Rome written the day after the society met at the Palazzo Borromini. In it he mentioned that he had met an interesting and intelligent young Englishwoman in the Forum that afternoon, and that he believed her to be one of the rare people blessed or cursed by the second sight. I admit that I was very excited to read it, for he had almost given up on his quest to find someone with the genuine talent to access the past."

His warm smile flashed again. "When Meg wrote to me that Alistair had fallen in love with a young Englishwoman he'd met in the Forum Romanum, I was certain the two were one and the same. Unless, of course, he had suddenly formed the habit of lurking about the place in hopes of meeting personable young Englishwomen."

Grace could have bitten her tongue. Hugh Kinsale hadn't known for sure, he'd merely been on a fishing expedition— and she had risen to the bait like a trout to a fly.

It was a moment before the rest of his words sank in. Alistair had *known*. He had always known.

She cast out a conversational lure of her own. "I see. Then this was something he had been searching for over some time."

"Oh, yes. The powers of the mind have always been an interest of his. He did not become obsessed with studying them, however, until after Finnula—" He broke off suddenly, two high spots of color in his cheeks.

"You needn't put on kid gloves with me," Grace said. "I am aware that my husband's late wife suffered under certain delusions. Although I have never exactly seen how my . . . special abilities, as you term them, have any bearing on her state of mind."

Hugh was taken aback. "Perhaps it is better if that information comes from Alistair himself. I am sure he has his reasons if he has not disclosed them to you."

"I see." She tried to appear calm although her spirits were extremely agitated. She couldn't get past the fact that all this time she had been trying to hide her unnerving abilities from her husband, and he already knew . . . No, it didn't make sense. Or did it? She had heard him speak several times, of how expectations colored observations. Of how volunteers in various experiments were often not informed—or misinformed—about the actual goals of those experiments.

She chose her words carefully. "What exactly did he tell you about me?"

"I am afraid that was the extent of it. And that he was due to leave Rome in a few days' time and regretted that there would not be sufficient time to persuade you to volunteer for his experiments in psychical research—he had something planned. I would not have been at all surprised to learn he had actually done so, however. Alistair is a very persuasive man. And an exceedingly determined one! I have never known him to fail in anything that really mattered to him. Obviously, he didn't expect your friendship to develop into a love match so rapidly at the time he wrote to me."

"No. Nor did I," she said slowly. She felt ill. As if she were smothering from the wild battering of her heart inside her chest. She had to get away somewhere to think.

The Reverend Kinsale didn't notice. His attention had been captured by the parlormaid standing in the open doorway. "Mr. McLean," she announced.

Grace looked up in a panic, expecting to see Alistair in the doorway. Wondering how she could meet his eyes without revealing her shock and outrage.

Instead it was Gordon McLean who strolled into the parlor. "Hugh! I saw the carriage and wondered if it could be you returned home. How good to have you back among us."

While they exchanged greetings, Grace took the opportunity to get a grip on her reactions. She still couldn't fathom all she'd just learned: Alistair had known from the very beginning that she had a strange talent to view the past. Why hadn't he said so?

She saw her happiness come tumbling down around her like one of Janet's houses built of cards. Alistair had not had the time to persuade her, so he had secured her interest in the only way possible: by marrying her.

She saw it all now with brutal clarity: the ride into the country, the visit to the dovecote. Their being locked in overnight. All of it engineered with one end—to ensure that she would have no choice but to put her trust into his hands.

To think I believed it was a kindly Fate that brought us together!

And that his interest in her had taken on more depth and meaning in recent weeks.

It was a bitter draught to swallow.

Gordon came to her side and took her hand. "How pale you are, my dear. I hope you are not coming down with the headache?"

She managed a wilted smile. "No. No. It is nothing, I assure you."

Both men scrutinized her, then looked away. Her face flamed as she realized what they were thinking: they suspected that she might be with child.

Good God! It was possible. She was several days overdue in her monthly cycle. *Not now,* she thought in perfect wretchedness. *Please, God, not now!*

Since Meg returned, followed by the maid with a tray of refreshments, there was no time for her to dwell on it. A quarter hour of agony passed by while the other three made pleasant conversation and she struggled to put in a comment from time to time. At the first moment politeness allowed, she rose.

"After Hugh's journey and your long separation, you cannot wish to entertain visitors," she said over Meg's protests. "Janet and I only intended to deliver the kitten. We must be on our way back to Rossmor."

"And I, as well. You will want to be alone with your family," Gordon added. "We will catch up on our news soon enough."

"At least let Janet stay a while," Meg pleaded. "She and the boys are having a great time, trailing a string for the kitten to chase. Let her sup with us and I'll have the groom take her back in the carriage later."

Meanwhile, Hugh and I can leave the three of them in care of the maid, and slip away to spend some time alone together.

Grace understood the unspoken words in Meg's eyes as clearly as though she'd said them aloud. She agreed to let Janet stay to dine with them, as much for her sake as anyone's. She couldn't decide if she wanted to confront Alistair without delay, or take some time to gather her shattered thoughts. Grace slipped on her cloak.

"I'll go out and tell her of your kind invitation."

Janet's cousins were delighted to learn she would take her supper with them. Grace was detained in the garden longer than she'd intended, as Angus and Geordie had to show her the gleaming wagon their father had brought home as a gift to them, and when she and Meg went back through the house, Hugh Kinsale was no longer in the parlor. Grace was relieved. She set off toward Rossmor in a state of agitation. All her niggling doubts regarding her marriage had crystalized into one dismaying truth: Alistair's reasons for marrying her had not been altruistic. He had served his own motives, although Grace wasn't sure what they might be.

As she rode through the wooded glen alone, she had the strong feeling that she was being watched. Grace glanced over her shoulder at the vicarage. The curtain had been pulled aside, and she wondered if it was Hugh standing there, looking after her. He was astute enough to know he'd said something to distress her; but of course he had no idea of what was actually—horribly—wrong.

She spurred her mount into a fast trot, and almost lost her hat when a sharp branch hit the crown with a snap. Grace straightened it, feeling the tight pull of her hairpins against her scalp. The headache she'd denied was fast becoming a reality. Her temple throbbed and burned.

Thunder echoed across the loch. She looked off to the mountains and saw swift dark clouds scudding in from the northeast. She kicked her horse into a gallop and raced the storm home, and she never once looked over to Freya's Tower.

As she reached the stables, Grace felt something brush her temple and the corner of her eye, like tiny wings. A freckle-faced young groom ran out to catch her reins. "Och, madam, what has happened? There's blood on your face!"

She touched a hand to her temple and looked at her tan glove. The fingertips were red with blood. She stared at it dully.

"It's nothing. I scraped my head against a branch cutting through the woods."

"You'd best have Mrs. Finley take a look at it."

"I will," she said, and let him help her dismount.

She went into the house and up the staircase without passing anyone. She had no desire to speak with Alistair until she thought out exactly what she intended to say. But when she pulled her hat off, a dark spot on the crown caught her eye. Grace touched it and her finger went through the neat bullethole. There was another on the opposite side, larger and slightly ragged.

She swayed as her vision dimmed, and crumpled to the floor.

When Grace came to, she was in her bedchamber with the curtains drawn. There was a sticking plaster at her temple and Alistair sat in the chair beside her, holding her hand. For several seconds she couldn't remember how she'd gotten from the vicarage parlor to Rossmor.

"How did I get here?"

His hand gripped hers. "You've had an accident, Grace. A poacher on the moors. You were exceedingly fortunate! His shot went wild but merely grazed your temple."

Grace closed her eyes as it all came back to her in a flood of pain and hurt and blazing white anger. She didn't trust herself to speak.

McLean lifted her hand and kissed her fingers. "If I find the villain responsible for this, I swear that I'll flay him alive with my own two hands!"

"Yes," she said, pulling away as her eyes flashed open again. "I can imagine you might. After all your careful plans and the deceit of luring me here to Rossmor, it would be a shame if death prevented me from my unwitting participation in your research experiments!"

He went very still. His eyes were alert and intense. "I won't pretend to misunderstand you," he said quietly.

Grace realized in that moment something she had always known on an instinctive level: her husband was a very dangerous man.

Chapter Twenty-three

Grace propped herself up against the pillows although her temple throbbed with the effort. It was nothing compared to the ache of her breaking heart. "You don't deny it, then. You brought me here for one reason only—because you believe that I may have abilities that reach beyond the normal human senses.

"I deny your implications," he said fiercely. "My interest in you was piqued by your unusual abilities—yes, I guessed something of them from the start—but the relationship that developed between us has nothing to do with that."

"Naturally, I see it quite otherwise. You took me to the dovecote planning that we would be forced to spend the night there." Her voice shook. "I was a fool to believe any of it."

He reached for her hand but she snatched it away.

"I swear on my soul that it was an accident—although I can see from the set of your face that you will never believe it now. I should like to know who has poisoned your mind against me."

She pushed her loose hair back from her face. "No one has 'poisoned' my mind. I can draw my own conclusions."

"What has this to do with anything, Grace? Devil take it, I married you to save your reputation, yes. But I must tell you I was not at all averse to the idea. I was attracted to you from the very start for reasons that had nothing at all to do with my research. And since that time, my feelings for you have grown so much stronger that I haven't dared admit to myself how deeply I care for you. Until now."

"How convenient that you should only just discover it," she said dryly. The effort of remaining calm had her fingernails digging deep into her palms. Inside she was bleeding.

His skin was flushed with anger. "You are being unfair. Would you have come away with me in Rome, if I had asked you to travel to Scotland in order to take part in my experiments? Because that was my original intention."

"Somehow you guessed that I am one of those people you have sought for your research."

"Yes. I will not lie to you. I realized in the Forum that you were in some sort of trance state—and that whatever you were experiencing affected you profoundly. I also realized that you saw things which I did not on our visit and unscheduled overnight stay at the dovecote. But don't you see that only enhanced my interest in you?"

Grace struggled to understand. "You brought me here hoping I would see something, either on my own or during the course of the séance. What was it, Alistair? At least tell me that. Tell me what was so important that you felt you had to dupe me?"

"I had several reasons—the first and foremost that I felt I had brought you to the brink of ruin through no fault of yours—or mine—and that it was my obligation as a gentleman to see you suffered no harm from it.

"Secondly, you are an intelligent and well-educated woman, with excellent powers of observation. I merely wanted any impression you received of Rossmor to be spontaneous and true. Untainted by expectations of what you might see or discover. It is the first rule of good science to conduct an experiment under controlled conditions, so that the conclusions drawn will not be colored by other factors."

His explanation made a lot of sense, which only made Grace angrier. "So you tricked me in the name of science? How noble!"

"What is the difference in my thinking you had a talent that might be useful to me, or in your thinking that a husband with private means and a large estate would make a marriage even more convenient?"

"How *dare* you!" Her hand arced out toward his cheek but he caught it and held both her hands firmly.

"You forget that we were almost strangers and that what we had initially was a contractual obligation to one another, not a love match. But I swear to God, Grace, I love you with more passion than I ever knew existed between a man and a woman!"

"This revelation has come upon you quite suddenly," she exclaimed.

"Don't be a little fool. I discovered it while we were on our honeymoon. But you gave me no hint that I had roused anything in you but your passions. If you think back over the course of the past two months, neither have you spoken words of love to me."

She couldn't refute his argument. Hot color rose in her cheeks. "It is difficult for a woman to be the first to speak out, especially given the circumstances. You are a gentleman and even if you felt trapped into marriage, you would not have shown it. As to myself, I imagined that you were well aware of my sentiments."

"How could I be, my dear, if you never spoke them?"

Her blush grew rosier. "I expected that my ardent responses to your lovemaking would be proof enough that my affections were deeply engaged."

McLean stared at her, and then began to laugh. "Oh, my delightful innocent!" He lifted her hand and kissed her fingers. "I forget that you have been sheltered from the world in many ways. I assure you that love and passion do not always go hand in hand. We, my darling, are two of the fortunate ones."

He leaned toward her and she breathed in his light cologne and the dearly familiar, masculine scent of him. But when he reached out to her, she held him back. "I believe there is something more to your story. I should like to hear it now."

"The experiment itself."

"Yes." She wrapped her arms around her knees. "Tell me everything."

He hesitated, frowning. "I must go back a considerable way. It is hard for me to say this. It has to do with Finnula, who is not here to defend herself."

"I understand you. Gordon hinted that the two of you were unsuited to one another, and that all had not been well between you at the time of her death."

"He was off the mark. It wasn't our marriage that was the problem, but her mental state. I loved Finnula and would have done anything I could to help her. She had always been . . . fey, I suppose is the best word. She was a girl of quicksilver moods. In the last year of her life there was more darkness in them than light.

"Finnula had a weakness of the mind, and had also suffered from headaches and nightmares for some time. She thought that she was going mad. She claimed to have seen the Gray Lady. That the ghost told her she would die and take its place. I feared her mind was deteriorating at a rapid rate."

Grace lifted her head. "I have heard voices, too. I have seen things. Do you think I am mad, also?"

"No." Alistair dragged his hand through his rumpled hair. "Neither do you smash every mirror in the house, or set fire to the curtains in your bedchamber. And slash your wrists and write vulgar words in blood upon the walls."

"Dear God!" Grace heard the flat hopelessness in his voice, and the hard ring of truth.

"I took her to Edinburgh to consult the finest doctors but her mind grew more anxious and less able to recognize reality. When we returned her condition worsened. For several weeks she was so bizarre and violent she had to be kept under lock and key. I tried every new cure or drug that offered hope. I brought experts in disorders of the brain and personality to visit her here. Finally, through the use of an Indian herb and Max Wundt's suggested treatment, she seemed to improve dramatically. I was encouraged enough to think the cure was permanent."

Grace's heart ached for him. "And it was not?"

"The lull before the storm. One winter afternoon I had estate business to attend to with my manager. Elspeth had gone out for a drive and Janet had been feverish earlier. Finnula promised to remain with her. When my business was concluded I went up to see how my daughter was faring. Her bed was empty and there was no sign of Finnula. I went below and Braedon told me they were in the drawing room."

His face grew grave. "The doors to the terrace stood open. There were fresh footsteps in the snow. Two sets of them. I found Janet lying outside the Old Hall. She was so cold and white that I thought she was dead. But when I lifted her in my arms she moaned and my heart lifted with hope. Another half hour and it would have been too late."

"How fortunate that you found her!"

"There were many anxious hours before we knew if she would recover without losing any fingers or toes due to frostbite. Days when her fever raged and I feared that lung fever would carry her off."

"But how did she get out there alone in the first place?"

"I believe that Finnula left her alone in the drawing room and went out into the snow. Janet followed her—that was apparent from their tracks—but she was wearing only a thin nightgown. She succumbed to the terrible cold before she reached the Old Hall."

"I see. But where was Finnula? Why had she gone and left Janet alone?"

He looked away. "I didn't know or care at the time. I didn't even look for her—and that is what I must live with now. At the time my anger was so white-hot I didn't dare face her with it, knowing how fragile her state of mind was."

"I cannot blame you for your anger. It was natural under the circumstances."

His eyes met hers. "It was more than anger. It was a black rage. I was afraid that I would throttle her with my bare hands! The next morning she was found lying dead among the rocks and ice at the foot of Freya's Tower out of remorse."

His mouth thinned. "Other people put a different interpretation on it. Some claimed that she was pushed over the parapet by the Gray Lady; others that it was I who sent her plunging to her doom."

Grace frowned. "A terrible tragedy. But what does this have to do with your research? Did you hope to contact Finnula's restless spirit?"

"No. It is Janet who concerns me now. You know of her dreams. But you don't know the rest of it. She believes that she is visited by a ghost, just as her mother claimed to be. The ghost of the Gray Lady of Rossmor."

"I still don't understand."

His eyes were stricken. "It was the need to uncover the truth that drove me. I had to find out—for Janet's sake. Has my daughter inherited her mother's hysterical personality—and potentially, her madness? Or could it be that Janet has the second-sight and 'sees' things in the same way that you do?"

"And if there is no ghost?" Grace asked softly.

"Then I would sell everything I have and travel to the

ends of the earth, until I found the cure to save her."

"I see. That is why you wanted to bring me here. To help you discover whether Janet's dreams and visions have a basis in madness or if she too has the power to look into the past."

"Yes. Will you help me, my love?"

Her answer was slow in coming. "Like you, Alistair, I will do anything I can. For Janet's sake."

"I knew I could count on your forgiveness, once you learned the truth." He reached out for her hand, but Grace pulled sharply away.

"You have my understanding," she said quietly, "but not my forgiveness. There should be no such secrets between man and wife. And I would have helped you willingly, as now, had I known the truth from the beginning. But this has placed a wedge between us. Trust is as fragile as a butterfly's wing. I will not give you mine again until I am more sure of you."

McLean's face went white. "I love you, Grace. You must believe me when I tell you that."

She shook her head. "How can I?"

He leaned forward, taking her face between his hands. "Then I shall woo you again, until I've won you." He leaned down as if to kiss her lips. Grace's hands splayed across his chest, pushing him away.

"You won't earn my trust by seducing me again, but by proving yourself worthy of it. Until that time," she told him, "I will sleep alone."

He rose, biting back the curse that rose to his lips. She was right. He had brought this down upon himself. "Very well. I'll have my valet move my things down the hall to my old suite of rooms. There will be talk among the servants, you realize."

"Yes. I'll tell Cait it is only until I'm recovered from

today's events." She looked away. "After a while they will become used to it."

McLean stopped and turned in the doorway. His eyes burned like dark blue flames in his strained face. "There will be no need. I'll win you back, Grace. I swear it!"

Chapter Twenty-four

Grace was luring a bright-eyed kitten across the drawing room with a length of red yarn, when the Reverend Hugh Kinsale was announced. He came into the room, his face furrowed with concern. When he saw her up and about, he looked taken aback.

"My dear! I am relieved to see you in such fine fettle," he said, striding across the room. "But should you be exerting yourself so soon after yesterday's mishap?"

"Between you and Alistair, you would have me wrapped up in cotton wool!" Grace smiled. "Even Elspeth is playing nursemaid today, plying me with possets and powders and cups of broth. I assure you—as I have them—that I am perfectly recovered, except for the slightest headache."

"Excellent news! Meg will be happy to hear it." He removed a folded square of paper, and a small stoppered vial from his pocket. "She sends her love in this note, and this headache potion that is guaranteed to banish all symptoms. A teaspoon of this in a bracing cordial or cup of hot tea, and you'll be right as rain."

"How kind of her! I wish she had come with you."

"We didn't know if you would be up to a visit. I have come by to consult your husband on a matter of business and promised to look in on you."

Grace thanked him. "I would enjoy her company greatly.

Please ask her to bring Angus and Geordie, as well. Janet found some of Meg's old toys while she was helping Mrs. Finley turn out the nursery cupboards, and we thought the boys would enjoy having them."

The butler returned with refreshments, and a book in a red leather slipcase. "Here is the volume you requested, madam."

"Thank you, Braedon." She took the book and invited Hugh to sit beside her. "Lady Helena sent this to me. I set it aside to peruse and then forgot all about it until a few minutes ago."

"Then let us have a cordial while you examine it," Hugh suggested. She let him pour a dollop of Meg's headache remedy into hers, then removed the book from its slipcase.

"Oh! *The Churches of Rome: An Illustrated Guide to Their History and Architecture.* I do hope it has an illustration of San Marcello al Corso, where Alistair and I were wed. It had the most amazing frescoes."

"I should like to see it." He sipped his drink and watched her while she found the index and went down it quickly. "Page forty-three," she said in triumph. But when she turned to the illustration it was totally unfamiliar to her. "How disappointing; this isn't it."

"But the caption," Hugh pointed out, "claims that it is. The name is very unusual—Saint Marcellus in the Thicket."

"Perhaps there is another of the same designation dedicated to him."

The preacher shook his head. "I don't believe that is possible within the same diocese. Perhaps you have confused the name. There are so many saints in the Church of Rome."

Grace laughed. "Lady Helena said something similar to me in Rome—but my Italian is quite good, I assure you. And you must allow that any woman would recall the name of the church in which she was wed. But this is clearly not the church where Alistair and I were married. It was much more intimate, and the frescoes were much more beautiful. Such gorgeous colors, enhanced with gold leaf."

She turned the page. "Ah! Here it is." She looked at the caption. "Stella Maris. Star of the Sea. How odd! They must have reversed the titles on the two illustrations."

Hugh Kinsale bent closer to the page. "But look—'Stella Maris' is written in the letters above the altar. And there in the fresco above the altar is the Virgin Mary as the Star of the Sea." He pointed to the footnote. "The church was deconsecrated in 1856. It is under renovation as a museum, to house the collection of Antonio Frascati, brother of Count Lorenzo Borromini."

Grace was dumbfounded. "But . . . I don't understand. It says quite clearly on our marriage certificate that the officiating priest was Brother Antonio and the church was San Marcello Al Corso."

She saw that he was staring at her. "What is it?"

The cleric rubbed a hand along his jaw. "He was not perhaps called *Padre* Frascati?"

"No. I am certain of it." She put her hand on Hugh's sleeve and lowered her voice. "Please! You must tell me what is wrong!"

"A brother is not a priest, but a layman," Hugh blurted out. "He cannot officiate at a marriage."

Grace felt the blood drain from her cheeks. "Then I have made a mistake," she said slowly. *A terrible mistake.*

She had looked at her marriage lines a hundred times. Or rather, what she had thought of as her marriage lines. They must be as false as the "priest" who had presided over the ceremony. As false as the man she called her husband had proven to be. Everything he'd told her yesterday—no, everything he'd told her from the very beginning, was nothing but a web of lies. And like a foolish dragonfly, she'd repeatedly stumbled into it, enmeshing herself in his plans.

She fought for control as her world crumbled around her.

"My dear Grace! You have gone white as flour. Let me ring for your maid."

"No, no! It is just a passing dizzyness," she protested. "I . . . I am quite all right."

Grace cocked her head, then jumped up so quickly the room spun. Hugh was there to grasp her arm. "Steady now! Really, Grace, you must go up to your room and rest."

She shook her head. "If I am not mistaken, that is Lady Helena Ainsley arriving from the train station in Inverness."

She went to the window and looked out in dismay. There would be no quick escape to her room now. A traveling carriage was pulled up in front of the door, with a second luggage vehicle holding an extremely elegant lady's maid and more luggage than she and Alistair both had taken along on their honeymoon. The groom opened the door and Lady Helena descended in an aubergine ensemble straight from the House of Worth.

To Grace's great surprise, a second woman exited the vehicle. The newcomer's head was averted, but she was stylishly dressed in a traveling outfit of bronze wool, with a matching hat perched upon her blond hair. She hadn't the faintest idea as to whom the woman might be.

A moment later the door opened and Braedon entered.

"Lady Helena Ainsley and Mrs. Dearing," he announced into the sudden silence.

The peeress swanned into the drawing room with the medium behind her. "I ran into Mrs. Dearing at the train station, and invited her to join me in the carriage. You do not mind to have two guests descend upon you a little early?"

Grace took her hands in hers. "Of course not! We are delighted to have you both with us." And she was. Anything to prove an added distraction. "Braedon, inform Mr. McLean that our guests have arrived, and have Mrs. Finley send in refreshments."

"Of course, madam." He bowed out of the drawing room

as Grace greeted Mrs. Dearing. "I understand we are to have a séance while you are with us. I hope you will not find it too exhausting."

The medium's blue eyes searched hers. "Not at all, my dear Mrs. McLean. I admit I am most eager to conduct it as soon as possible."

"Excellent," Lady Helena proclaimed.

"I am also looking forward to the seance. Your reputation is well known to me, Mrs. Dearing," said Hugh.

"You are very kind," the medium said with a small smile. "I am afraid that our host is not convinced of my talents," she said. "I hope to win him over during my stay."

Grace's mind was in utter turmoil. *Alistair deceived me. Dear God, what am I to do?* Her good breeding came to the rescue. "It is a long journey from the train station to Rossmor. Let me take you up to your rooms so that you might refresh yourselves and rest before dinner."

Lady Helena waved her hand airily. "I am sure Mrs. Dearing would be glad of a rest. You must take her up straightaway, Grace. However, I wish to visit with Hugh a while longer."

"Of course. Mrs. Dearing?"

"I should like nothing better than a cup of tea and a nap," the unexpected guest confessed.

Grace led her up to the Gold Bedchamber, which was in the medieval wing of the house. She was still unsteady on her feet but managed her duties as hostess well enough. Mrs. Dearing took in the latticed windows, the high carved bed with its gold and crimson hangings, and the gilded mirror over the fireplace with approval.

"Charming. Quite charming. And very atmospheric! I am so glad I have come to Rossmor, Mrs. McLean."

"As are we to receive you," Grace murmured. She pulled aside a curtain to reveal a tastefully furnished dressing area. "And here is the bell cord, should you require anything.

I'll ring for one of the maids to bring water and help you out of your traveling garments."

"In a moment. But first I should like a word with you in private." The medium shut the door and all her feigned weariness was gone. She turned to Grace briskly. "Be careful to whom you give your trust," she said. "I have received a message for you from beyond the veil. You are in very great danger!"

"Danger?" Grace was taken aback. "From whom?"

"I am not certain, so I will say no more at the moment."

"Perhaps you are a bit late with your warning." Grace gave a shaky laugh. "It was yesterday that I was grazed by a poacher's bullet."

Mrs. Dearing shook her head. "There is worse to come."

Impatience burned in Grace's breast, masking the fear. "If you have something specific to tell me, I would appreciate it. However, I am not interested in vague mumbo-jumbo."

"That is a very strange thing for you to say, Mrs. McLean, when you and I share something in common. Yes," she went on, as Grace's eyes widened. "I know that you are, like myself, a 'sensitive.' Your gift is raw and untrained, but it is very strong. Like a sword, it can cut both ways. If you do not learn to harness it sufficiently, you could suffer great harm."

Grace took a deep breath, trying to ease the hammering of her heart. "I see. And this is the danger of which you speak?"

"No, my dear. You are in peril from forces around you. She says that she has been trying to warn you and that you have sensed her presence on several occasions."

"She?" Grace asked the question, although she already knew the answer. "Who is it who has told you this?"

Mrs. Dearing sighed. "A woman who went over to the other side before her time. She claims that she was once—as you are now—mistress of Rossmor. Her name is Finnula."

Chapter Twenty-five

The maid came in response to Grace's tug on the bellpull, and she left Mrs. Dearing to her ministrations. On the way back she saw the door to the estate room was ajar. McLean looked up as she entered. "My dear, you should be resting."

"We have guests," she said. "Hugh Kinsale is in the drawing room with Lady Helena—and Mrs. Dearing is upstairs recruiting her strength after the journey."

"What do you think of her?"

"I have not come to discuss Mrs. Dearing," Grace said coldly. "I have come to tell you that I am leaving you."

He stared at her. "What nonsense is this?"

"What nonsense was that in Rome?" she demanded. "A deconsecrated church, a false priest, and a certificate of a sham marriage!"

He didn't deny it. His blue eyes regarded her warily, and she sensed his mind racing, wondering the best way to handle the situation.

This was his worst nightmare come true. McLean knew he couldn't bluff his way out of it. "Perhaps it is best that everything is out in the open. I am sorry that you have found out in this way. Indeed, I had hoped you never would."

The moment the words were out he wished that he could

call them back. They were rusted nails in the coffin of his hopes.

Grace felt ill. She realized that, on some level, she had hoped he would not only deny everything, but produce evidence to convince her otherwise. The pain of his betrayal was so overwhelming she could scarcely bear up beneath its weight.

"My God, Grace! Don't look at me as if I were a monster! I did what I had to do to save your reputation. If we could have been married in Rome in time, I would have moved heaven and earth to do it. It was impossible under the circumstances. That is why I'd spoken to you of repeating our vows before Hugh. We would have been properly married and you none the wiser for it."

"Oh, I am wise now," she said bitterly.

He came around the desk. "We'll say our vows before Hugh, I swear it! Tomorrow, if you like, and make our union legal in the eyes of God and the law. But vows or no, Grace, you are my wife!"

"I thought I was," she whispered. "But you made me your *whore*!"

He went white. "No! I love you, Grace. I swear it! I would do anything if we could go back in time and begin anew . . ."

"Ah, so would I!" she cried, turning away. "Anything that would have kept me from such folly. I wish I had never met you!"

"Wait! You cannot leave without hearing what I have to say. You owe me at least that."

Fury poured through her. "Don't," she said. "I cannot bear it. I have listened to enough of your lies. I owe you nothing! Everything I thought you gave me was an illusion. You, who took me out to the island in the loch, and preached to me of loyalty! This was the ultimate betrayal. A sham marriage, a travesty of love!"

He reached out and caught her wrists in his iron grip.

She wrenched her hands away. "Don't touch me! Don't ever touch me again!"

"Grace!"

"I will stay until the séance. For Janet's sake. You will never see me again."

She ran from the room as if fleeing a plague. He stood there, haggard and worn, but made no attempt to follow her. He knew that there was nothing he could ever do or say to win her back.

Grace went back to her room in a daze. She locked the door, then went to the one leading into the sitting room and slid that bolt home, too. If she had the strength she would have begun packing the few things she intended to take with her, but she couldn't even attempt it. A strange lassitude had come over her and the room looked—*strange.*

The walls seemed to move in and out with her heartbeat. *Almost,* she thought, *as if they are breathing!*

A moment later she was stumbling toward the basin, where she was horribly ill. She retched until she brought up nothing but bitter bile. Once it was over with, she felt better. After rinsing her mouth and washing her face, she made her way to the bed and laid down upon the quilt and closed her eyes.

Her lids were so heavy she couldn't lift them. Not when she heard the voice whisper her name or felt cool fingers brush lightly over her forehead. So lightly that it might have been nothing but her imagination.

Or perhaps a bit of trailing mist.

Chapter Twenty-six

Dinner was an informal and extremely strained affair. Meg and Gordon and Lady Helena tried to carry on the conversation over the medallions of pheasant and rack of lamb, with scant help from the rest. Mrs. Dearing was preoccupied, Hugh distressed. McLean and Grace were like mannequins, moving and speaking and all of it just the pulling of strings.

She could scarcely look at him. The man she had grown to love and trust, who had betrayed her so cruelly. The man who knew every inch of her body so intimately, and so wantonly.

It was difficult to meet the others' eyes as well—as if she feared they would see "harlot" written in scarlet letters across her forehead. Hugh knew or guessed enough, that was evident. He hadn't shared his discovery with either Meg or Lady Helena. It was plain that they were both perplexed. She wondered if she should write a note to Meg before she left Rossmor, explaining her reasons, and decided it was better not to attempt it. What could she say? Nothing would make it right.

Janet was another matter. Grace had felt such a pang when the girl had kissed her good-night, knowing they would soon be parted. Heaven only knew what excuse Alistair would make up to explain her departure to his daughter. *No doubt he will come up with some plausible lie.* It broke her heart to think of it.

After the dessert course was removed, Grace rose and led the ladies from the room. Braedon hovered outside the drawing room to intercept them. "If it pleases you, madam, Mr. McLean has arranged for a fire to be lit in the solar. We are instructed to bring the tea cart there later."

Lady Helena clapped her hands. "How delightful! I love the solar, and it is so rarely used for entertaining."

Grace was a little startled but led her guests through to the older wing. The lamps had been lit in the Old Hall and they went up the stairs, past the gallery, and into the cozy room. Flames leapt high in the hearth, chasing away the evening chill. She saw that extra chairs had been brought in and set around the table where Janet liked to play at building her card houses.

Mrs. Dearing smiled. "I see your husband is wasting no time in putting my talents to the test, Mrs. McLean."

"What do you mean?"

Lady Helena laughed. "My dear Grace, it appears we are going to have a séance!"

He is as anxious to be rid of me as I am to go, Grace thought. She strolled around the room, with its ancient tapestries and old court cupboard. *Strange to think that this is the last time I shall ever be in this room.*

Lady Helena did a turn about the chamber. "How easy it is to imagine that we are back in time three hundred years."

The medium nodded but was rather distracted. "What is that lovely scent?" she asked finally. "I smell lavender and—I think—rose. But what is the other fragrance blended with it?"

At first Grace didn't smell anything but the woodsmoke on the hearth. Then it grew around her like a cloud of mist and she recognized it. It was the scent that accompanied the voice and the visions. Finnula's potpourri. She shivered.

It was Meg who answered. "It is bergamot," she said slowly. "It has been many years since I've smelt it, but it is unmistakable. I have never cared for the combination, but Finnula used it for her own perfume and sachets. She claimed to have re-created it from an old recipe handed down from Freya."

"Finnula had a talent for such things," Lady Helena remarked. "I remember that Gordon used to bring her all sorts of scented oils and exotic herbs for her potpourri and tonics, and clever glass bottles from Egypt and India. Alas, I never had the knack for mixing them. Hers were light and elegant, while mine always came out smelling like a chemist's shop—or worse. Once I mixed too much civet and we had to air the stillroom out for days."

The men arrived, fresh from a round of port. "I hear we are to have a séance tonight," said Hugh.

"Bah!" Gordon laughed. "Table-tapping and tipping! It is all done with accomplices and cymbals sewn to . . . ah, one's clothing."

"You needn't be afraid to say 'garters' in our presence," Helena chided. "We are not children. And I doubt if any of us will have accomplices here. Most especially Mrs. Dearing, who is the only one of us who is not related in some way."

Mrs. Dearing smiled. "Very graciously said, Lady Helena. Thank you."

McLean herded them over to the table. "Let us try our luck at raising the spirits," he said. "Then you may ask them if *they* have cymbals on their garters."

But Gordon had drawn Elspeth away from the others. "Something is wrong between Alistair and Grace."

"Nonsense!"

"Earlier today I dropped by to speak with Alistair. They were in the estate room, quarreling rather violently."

Elspeth looked shocked. "I didn't know you were the sort of person to listen at keyholes, Gordon!"

"You know damned well that I am not. A deaf man would have heard the raised voices. I couldn't tell what they were saying, but Grace fled the room looking distraught." He rubbed his jaw. "And one of the servants told me that he has moved out of their room."

"Servants' gossip!" Elspeth's voice rang with disdain. "Grace was almost shot by a poacher yesterday as she rode home from the vicarage. It was a very near thing. Alistair slept in another room out of consideration for her rest."

Gordon smiled and gave a gusty sigh of relief. "I hadn't heard. That explains it, then. But the valet said he'd taken all his belongings with him, and I jumped to the conclusion that they were estranged. I couldn't imagine any other reason for him to do so."

Lights of excitement danced in Elspeth's eyes. "Can't you? I can think of one very good reason. Alistair has always wanted a houseful of children, and you know that poor Finnula suffered several miscarriages. Perhaps Grace is in an interesting condition." She smiled happily. "Time will tell if I am right or not."

"Right about what?" Hugh had come up beside them.

"Elspeth thinks there may soon be the announcement that a new little McLean is coming into the world."

"Well, well, well!" Hugh glanced back at Grace. "I hadn't even considered the possibility."

Lady Helena rose from her chair and went to them. "You are slippery as eels. Everytime we try to get everyone seated, someone slips away." She tucked one arm through Gordon's and the other through Hugh's. "Now you have no choice but to come with me, or be excessively rude!"

Everyone laughed and they went to take up their places at the table.

McLean was edgy. He didn't want anything to go wrong, and tried to work it so Grace was at his right side. She eluded him, and took up her place almost opposite, with Hugh on one side and Mrs. Dearing on the other.

McLean was displeased, but took Lady Helena on his right with Gordon beside her, and Meg on his left.

"Do we turn out the lights and hold hands?" Lady Helena asked.

"That is the accepted mode," Mrs. Dearing replied.

"Then we will link hands first," McLean announced, "so there is no question of anyone holding a stuffed glove in the darkness. I will have Braedon put out the lamps before he leaves."

A expectant silence fell over the little group as they held hands. Braedon tiptoed around the room. One by one the lamps were snuffed. The only light was the red-gold glow from the hearth, but even the flames had been banked. At Mrs. Dearing's request a screen was placed in front of it.

"I do not know if my guide will come tonight," she announced. "However, even should he not make an appearance, I will still receive messages from the spirit world. Open your minds, and close your eyes . . ."

Grace closed her eyes with the others, then peeked out beneath her lashes. The chamber was very dark. She could barely discern the outlines of the people sitting around the circular table.

"Now we will remain silent," Mrs. Dearing said, "while I summon my guide. Do not break the contact except under the most dire circumstances! I have no desire to be left wandering about an astral plane, with no way of returning." After a good deal of shifting about and clearing of throats, the medium began.

"There are two spirits here," she said in a voice that seemed somehow altered. "Both women. One is the guardian spirit of this place. She cannot see us nor we, her. The spirit is benevolent. The other one is trying to communicate. I can feel her trying to enter my body. Mr. Kinsale . . . You must play the part of interlocutor . . ."

Mrs. Dearing's voice trailed off.

Grace could hear the susurrus of her blood moving in

her veins and arteries. It grew from the rustling of silk and satin to the loud beating of wings, then fell into profound silence.

"Who is there?" Hugh asked firmly. "Will you speak to us?"

There was only rustling silence and the crackle of the fire. "Who are you?" he asked again. "Speak! I command you. What is it you wish to tell us?"

The answer came low and full. "Murder . . ."

"What is your name?"

There was no answer. "I command you to speak your name," Hugh said.

Lady Helena leaned forward. "Ask it if Freya . . ."

The voice that spoke was soft, yet echoing. *"I am not Freya, although she is here among us . . . I am Finnula!"*

"Finnula! Why are you here?" McLean's voice was ragged. "What is it you want of us?"

"Justice!"

A tremor ran through the linked hands but no one let go. "Justice for what?" Lady Helena asked breathlessly.

The voice was cool and distant, but filled with arcane power. *"For my death. I did not jump from Freya's Tower . . . He lifted me over the parapet, dashed me to the rocks below . . ."*

"Seek your vengeance. Name your murderer!" Hugh exclaimed.

"Vengeance . . . yes. He is here among you tonight . . ."

There was a sharp rap and the table lifted, then twisted violently sideways. A woman screamed. Chairs scraped back on the ancient floor and there was a good deal of shouting and confusion. Someone hurried to light the lamps.

When they were lit, only two people were still seated at the table: Mrs. Dearing was slumped forward, her head resting on her arms. Grace was rigid, her eyes staring, and it was from her lips that the voice of Finulla was issuing.

"I will tell you his name that you may bring him to justice. It was . . ."

The table took a big jump sideways and tipped over. McLean grabbed Grace and lifted her out of the way. He carried her to the settee and knelt beside her.

"Grace! Grace, wake up, my love!"

She came to slowly. Her head seemed filled with fog. Meg and Elspeth leaned over her anxiously, while Lady Helena issued orders to Hugh and Gordon. "Gordon, ring for Braedon and Mrs. Finley."

"What . . . what has happened?" Grace asked dazedly. "Why are we in the solar?"

"We were conducting a séance, darling. You fell into a trance state," McLean said. "I thought it was a trick, that Mrs. Dearing was pretending that she'd been taken over by a spirit from beyond."

"Then—was it trickery or was it real? Did she contact someone from beyond the veil?"

He held her hands tightly in his. "Finnula spoke to us," he said gravely. "Her voice was unmistakable. But she did not speak through Mrs. Dearing, love. She spoke through you."

Meg stood up. "Where is Mrs. Dearing? She seems to have vanished!"

It was only then, that Hugh spied the medium on the floor between the table and the wall. "She appears to have fainted!"

Lady Helena bent over the woman, saw the thick wet blood that mingled freely with Mrs. Dearing's pale hair, and straightened up with a most inelegant shriek.

"Mrs. Dearing is injured! Send for the surgeon down in the village."

"Better yet," Gordon said, "I'll fetch him myself. My new team can cover the ground twice as quickly."

But McLean had left Grace's side to kneel beside the medium. He placed his fingers over the pulse spot at her throat. "I am afraid there is no need for the surgeon. She's dead."

Chapter Twenty-seven

It was a subdued party that sat in the drawing room as the clock struck eleven. Grace was stunned, Meg in tears, and Lady Helena, for once, silenced. Hugh sat beside his wife, holding her hand.

"She must have slipped and hit her head on that marble statue during the commotion," he said for the fifth time.

"That poor woman, come all this way to suffer such a tragedy!" Elspeth said.

They heard carriage wheels on the drive, and Braedon entered solemnly to announce that the vicarage carriage was ready, and Mr. Gordon McLean's, as well.

"I don't feel that I should leave you," Meg said.

"Nonsense," Lady Helena said, regaining her assertiveness. "You need to be under your own roof with your children tonight."

Hugh led his wife out. "If you need anything, you only have to send for me and I shall come, no matter the hour."

Grace nodded. "Thank you. I shall let you know what the arrangments are tomorrow."

She escorted them to the drawing room door. "Where is Gordon?"

"Off conferring with Alistair, I believe. I'll go and see what is keeping them."

She went up the staircase toward the small bedroom

where Mrs. Dearing had been laid out. Gordon McLean
came along the corridor to join her. "Excellent timing," he
said. "I was just coming in search of you. Janet had a ter-
rible nightmare. The maid left her to fetch a glass of warm
milk—and when she came back, Janet was gone!"

"Rouse the servants! We'll search the house . . ."

"Calm down. Alistair has already given the orders. You
had best go back to your guests."

"No, I must help find her. Poor child, she'll be fright-
ened to death."

The words had an ominous chill after the evening's
events.

"Then I'll go with you."

"Look!" Grace pointed to where a tapestry billowed in
the draft. "The door to the medieval wing is open. She must
have gone there. When she's upset, she goes to the so-
lar . . ."

They raced along the corridor and into the gallery above
the Great Hall. Grace couldn't shake the uncanny sensation
of being followed. It didn't take long to figure out where
the girl was headed. The door to Freya's Tower stood open
and an icy draft swirled through the air.

"Oh, how cold it is here," Grace gasped. She felt as if
she'd been plunged into a vast pool of ice. The warmth was
sucked from her very bones, and she found her limbs re-
sponding awkwardly when she needed to be swift and sure.

"It is the shock that makes you feel the cold so," Gordon
told her. "Stay here where it's safe and warm. I'll find Janet
if she's up here, and bring her down!" He vanished into
the ascending darkness.

Grace hesitated.

Grace.

"Yes?" She glanced over her shoulder, thinking Elspeth
had called her. There was nothing behind her but shadows.
She couldn't bear to stand waiting to know if Janet had

gone up to the ramparts, and followed Gordon. She could hear his footsteps echoing above.

Grace. Go back!

She whirled around. Still nothing. *It is my imagination*, she told herself. But with every step the sensation that she was not wanted here grew stronger.

"I see her!" Gordon called out. "By the battlements. No, Janet! No!"

Grace raced up the last of the circular steps after him. At the top of the stairs the open door showed a rectangle of stars half-obscured by mist. As she approached it, the mist thickened. Coalesced into a moving, luminous fog. A woman formed of light, the details of her garments barely discernible. Only enough to show that it was not a flowing gown she wore, but a winding sheet.

The shrouded figure blocked the way, and Grace was almost paralyzed with terror. *Go back! Grace . . .*

"No!"

A high-pitched scream from beyond the door galvanized her. Gathering her courage, Grace forced her way through the luminous mass and came out onto the top of Freya's Tower.

Gordon stood near the edge of the battlements, his hands reaching out toward Janet. Grace could see the fabric of her white nightgown reflecting the starlight. But when she arrived at the spot there was no sign of Janet. A piece of white cloth fluttered in the breeze.

"Why, it's nothing but a bit of lace curtain . . . Why on earth would anyone put it here?"

"I did," Gordon said. "To lure you up here."

"But . . . why?"

"It is nothing personal, my dear. I am quite fond of you. But I find myself in dire financial straits, and there is only one way out of it. Someone must die—and I really would rather it isn't me."

Grace bit her lip. He looked the same except for his eyes.

They were the eyes of a madman. "What have you done with Janet?"

"Nothing that will harm her. She is safe enough, drugged and sleeping in one of the empty guest rooms. Don't worry, I was careful not to give her too much. She'll be fine in the morning after a good night's sleep."

Grace whirled on him. "What? Are you insane?"

Alistair stepped between them. "I am afraid that he is. Insane with jealousy! He has always coveted Rossmor. Until tonight I didn't realize that he wanted it badly enough to commit murder—again! It was you who aggravated Finnula's mental problems, whispering through the old speaking tubes your father put in. Putting drugs in her tonics. It was you who lured her up to the tower—and pushed her over. What was the rest of your plan?"

"I really underestimated the power of your reputation," Gordon replied suavely. "I expected that you would be arrested and hanged for her murder. And then little Janet and her fortune would be in my hands. I didn't mean for her to become ill, you know. I'm very fond of her."

Alistair had been moving closer as he listened. Suddenly he stepped in front of Grace. "Run! Head for the other turret!"

"It's locked from the inside," Gordon said, pulling a dueling pistol from his pocket. "This is loaded and on a hair trigger. From your own gunroom, Alistair. Don't try anything foolish. You might get hurt."

"I don't imagine either of us is intended to get down from here alive in any case."

"You were always quick-witted, nephew. Perhaps you think that you know everything?"

McLean edged slowly away from Grace. "I know that you are deeply in debt. I know that you were always upset that Rossmor and all its lovely collections and lands came to me. And that my mother's uncle left me his fortune from his inventions, as well."

"It is highly unfair that you should have both. You've had them quite long enough. I had only intended to dispose of your bride tonight, but this strange affair of your marriage—or shall I say non-marriage—gives me the perfect excuse to accelerate my plans. How distraught I shall be at your deaths. Murder and suicide," he said calmly. "The only quandary is which of you should be which?"

"And what of my daughter?" McLean said raggedly. "How do you intend to dispose of her?"

"You forget. Janet doesn't come into her majority until the age of twenty-five, according to your will—and I am named her trustee in it. That gives me sufficient time to bring myself about."

McLean regarded him stonily. "And what then? Will you dispose of her as you did her mother?"

"So you have guessed that, too." He shook his head. "I wanted no more heirs to Rossmor clouding my future. I have no children of my own, other than a natural son who emigrated to Canada—a most expensive and unsatisfactory lad! He has been a drain on my purse. On the other hand, I have always been exceedingly fond of Janet. If I succeed in putting my affairs in good order, there might be no need to ever consider an act which I would find extremely distressful."

"Noble of you!" Grace snapped.

Gordon rounded on her. "You may be as sarcastic as you like, my dear, but it will not be for long. The rain will fall soon—and so will you! Your body will be found upon the rocks at the foot of the tower. Just like Finnula. But this time there will be no doubt in anyone's mind of Alistair's guilt in either case."

She fought against the sickening sensation his words wrought in her. "You're mad. There is no way you can throw me off and place the blame upon my husband—and then dispose of him, too."

"Can't I?"

"He is younger and stronger than you," Grace said. "You cannot hope to throw him over the tower as easily."

"Alistair," Gordon pronounced airily, "will kill himself in remorse after your battered body lies bleeding upon on the rocks."

"He would never do that!"

"Perhaps not in actuality. But I assure you that people will be convinced that he did." Gordon smiled. "Especially when he is found with a bullet through his head—and his gun beside him."

Alistair laughed. "It won't happen that way. I will distract him, Grace, while you run back the way we came. I can hold him that long."

Gordon was enraged. "You fool! What is to prevent me from shooting you and her both!"

In the moonlight Alistair's face was a silver mask, his eyes gleaming diamonds. "The fact that a dueling pistol has only one shot in it!"

He launched himself at the other man. "Run, Grace!"

She was too stunned to move for a few vital seconds. A shot rang out. "No! *Alistair!*" He fell heavily against the parapet and Gordon lunged toward him. McLean managed to roll and throw the other man off, but the odds were against him, wounded as he was. His shoulder gleamed wetly in the starlight.

Instead of running for the door, she ran toward the two figures grappling against the ramparts. She looked around for the stout stick that normally propped the heavy door open. It had grown very dark as the clouds moved in, but the moon suddenly revealed itself in a wash of pale light.

The stick lay to one side. Grace grabbed it up in two hands, and entered the fray. She would never know for sure if Alistair could have saved himself. He had Gordon by the throat, but the older man had the advantage—blood drenched the side of Alistair's shirt.

Without stopping to think, Grace lifted the heavy piece

of wood and swung it two-handed, like a warrior queen wielding a battle sword. The whirling blackthorn stick hit Gordon's shoulder and the side of his face with a sickening thud just as McLean lurched to his feet. He grasped at his uncle's arm as the older man's body crumpled against the parapet.

It was all so fast she could never recall exactly what happened next. One moment there were three of them upon the ramparts of Rossmor, the next only two. Gordon McLean had tumbled backward over the edge of the tower, his jacket billowing out like the wings of a great black bird as he fell to the rocks below.

Braedon came running up onto the battlements, with Hugh and several of the menservants. They were met by a shocking sight: Grace kneeling in a pool of spreading dark liquid, beside McLean's still form.

Hugh ran to them. "What in God's name has happened here?"

"There has been an accident," she said shakily. She knelt beside Alistair's still form. She knew then that she loved him with an undying passion. He had done what he had done to save his daughter. And he had risked his life—or even rendered it up—to save her.

She could no longer doubt his love.

"But where is Gordon?" Lady Helena exclaimed.

"He has fallen from the tower," Grace answered.

"Great heavens. He'll never have survived the fall!"

"No. He has gone the route he intended for me."

Grace took charge. "Braedon, have Mrs. Finley meet us in the master chamber with bandages and hot water. Hugh, help Braedon carry Alistair to our bedchamber."

Alistair opened his eyes and looked up at her. "Don't leave me, Grace."

She cradled his head against her breast. "I never will, my darling. I swear it."

"I shall hold you to your promise," he said with a weak smile, and passed out in her arms.

Epilogue

Meg and the twins sat at one end of the drawing room at Rossmor, working a wooden puzzle with Janet. Beyond the open terrace doors, the glen was in bloom, and across the room Grace reclined on the sofa with an open book on her lap, watching Elspeth read her mail.

Grace couldn't stand it any longer: "I hope that Count Borromini is well?"

"Quite well," Elspeth said, and kept reading. But two spots of high color rose on her cheeks.

Grace and Meg exchanged glances. Count Borromini had joined them the day following the double tragedy at Rossmor, and had stayed on to comfort them. He and Elspeth had struck up a great friendship over the course of his stay. Ever since, letters had been traveling back and forth between Rossmor and London, where the count had taken a large house just outside London, much to the surprise of his relations in Rome.

Meg smiled. "I wonder how long he intends to remain in England?"

Elspeth's blush deepened. "At least to the end of June. He intends to invite us all to be his guests after Easter Week. Do you think Alistair would consent to go?"

He came in through the terrace doors. "Go where?"

"To London at month's end, as the guests of Count Borromini."

"Good Lord! Lorenzo knows how I hate leaving Rossmor at this time of year!"

Elspeth's gasp of dismay made him laugh. "I am only teasing you, my dear cousin. He has already written to me, inviting us to stay a few weeks with him. I think it would be very good for all of us. I know your aversion to London, however, so you need not accompany us if you don't wish to do so, Elspeth."

Her face went from red to white. Then McLean took pity on her. "I am teasing you again, Elspeth. Grace and I have every intention of accepting his kind offer." His smile flashed, tinged with affection and a touch of mischief. "After all, we would not want to blight your chances of becoming a countess."

Elspeth rose with great dignity and opened her mouth to make a cutting retort. Instead she hesitated and blushed again. "I . . . I do think he is inclined to favor my company," she said awkwardly, sounding like a young girl in the throes of her first love. "However, only a fool would read anything into it!"

"My dear Elspeth," McLean said, "I am no fool. The man is head over heels. If he doesn't come up to scratch, I shall horsewhip him through Trafalgar Square!"

It was even odds as to whether Elspeth would laugh or stalk off in a temper. "Leave her alone, Alistair," Grace said. "She has no need of you to champion her." Meg exchanged another look with Grace and her brother. Elspeth kept her own counsel, but they both believed that there would be an announcement, in the very near future, that she was going to become the Countess Borromini. Grace realized that she would miss her dreadfully. *What a difference a few months can make!*

Alistair came over to his wife and kissed her cheek. "Have you told Janet and Meg's monsters the news?"

"Your father and I wish very much that we could have had you and the rest of the family with us in Rome. Since you were not, we are going to renew our vows at St. Declan's at the end of the month."

"Will it be like a wedding?"

McLean smiled at Grace, then kissed his daughter. "Exactly so, my darling girl. Now that our six months of mourning is over, we will do it up in style. And you and Angus and Geordie will all be members of the wedding party."

Janet laughed and clapped her hands in excitement. "Angus and Geordie will be our ring-bearers," Grace explained as the twins listened eagerly, "and each will carry a pillow with one of the rings down the aisle for us to exchange during the vows."

"If they don't stick them in their ears, or drop them down a drain, or lose them outside the church," Alistair interjected.

Everyone laughed. Grace saw the look of excited expectancy on Janet's face. "And you shall be the flower girl," she told Janet. "Elspeth is making you a dress of white silk trimmed with silver embroidery and blue ribbons, to match your eyes. And you shall have a chaplet of matching silk flowers on your hair, and a posy in a silver holder."

Janet laughed and clapped her hands. "And will there be a party after, with dancing in the Old Hall, and all the neighbors and servants in attendance?"

"If you wish," Grace told her, smiling. "And you may stay up until midnight if you like."

Janet threw her arms around Grace. "Oh, thank you, Mama!"

It was the first time Janet had ever called her that, and Grace's eyes sparkled with happy tears. McLean came to their side and kissed them both. "With apologies to Meg, but I shall have the most beautiful ladies of all at my side."

His eyes met Grace's. "Always and ever," she said. They

had started anew from that horrible night in the tower. Now the foundation of their marriage would be based on love and truth. And loyalty.

McLean turned to answer a question from one of the twins and Janet danced away to play with the kitten again.

The sunshine grew brighter on the far side of the room, where Grace had ordered Finnula's portrait to be put back in its original place. She glanced up at it as the light grew to an almost blinding brilliance that seemed to sparkle as if it were filled with tiny, glowing stars.

No one else seemed to notice anything. Grace looked at Finnula's portrait and realized that the menacing shadows were gone. The young woman in the painting no longer looked fearful, but content. At peace.

Grace . . .

She heard her name called clearly, but this time there was no fear in her. Rising, she went toward the portrait, stepping into the circle of golden light.

It is time for me to leave. Take care of Janet. She is your daughter now . . .

"I shall. Good-bye, Finnula," Grace whispered. "Godspeed—and safe journey home."

The light flared to incredible brilliance and winked out, and nothing but sunshine—and the warmth in Grace's heart—remained.

McLean came over to her. "Talking to yourself, love?"

"No. I was saying good-bye to Finnula. She is gone now. She is at peace."

He smiled and pulled her into his arms, ignoring the interested stares of his young nephews, and kissed her soundly. "So am I, my dearest love. So am I."